IS ORIGINAL SIN IN SCRIPTURE?

IS ORIGINAL SIN
IN SCRIPTURE?

HERBERT HAAG

translated by Dorothy Thompson

with an Introduction by
BRUCE VAWTER, C.M.

SHEED AND WARD : NEW YORK

Contents

Abbreviations

Bb	*Biblica*
D	Denzinger, *Enchiridion Symbolorum* (bis 31. Aufl.)
DBS	*Dictionnaire de la Bible,* Supplement
DS	Denzinger, *Enchiridion Symbolorum*, 32. Aufl. hrg. von A. Schonmetzer (Freiburg i. Br. 1963)
DThC	*Dictionnaire de Theologie Catholique*
EvTh	*Evangelische Theologie*
LThK	*Lexikon fur Theologie und Kirche*, 2. Aufl. (1957–1965)
MuThZ	*Munchener Theologische Zeitschrift*
NewTestSt	*New Testament Studies*
NRTh	*Nouvelle Revue Theologique*
RScR	*Recherches de Science Religieuse*
Schol	*Scholastik*
ThQ	*Tubinger Theologische Quartalschrift*
VT	*Vetus Testamentum*

7

Introduction

Revelation, the response to which is faith, has its one source in the word of God. This word, addressed to the People of God which it has called into being, is encountered where this people has its "place" in the world, namely, in the church. It is encountered in the church's liturgy and preaching, in its sacramental ministry and teaching. Above all, it is encountered in the scripture, which the church, "taught by the Holy Spirit, day by day strives to understand more deeply, that she may continuously feed her children with the divine word." (Constitution *Dei Verbum,* art. 23.)

Theology, which may still be adequately described as "faith seeking understanding," has many sources because the sources of understanding are many. The understanding of the adult is not that of the child, though the faith of the one may be that of the other. The understanding of twentieth-century man is not that of mediaeval man, though both may have a single creed. Both in the adult as contrasted with the child, and in modern man with the Christian of the middle ages, a broadening of the sources of information and thus of understanding has taken place. It is as natural to grow and to change in the understanding of one's faith as it is to grow and to change in the understanding of every other aspect of one's life. What is unnatural is to arrest the process of growth and change, or to permit it to atrophy. There may be great virtue in "a childlike faith," but if by this expression we mean—as too frequently we do—a childlike understanding of faith, it implies no virtue at all, except for a child. An adult with a childlike understanding of anything at all is to that extent a retarded person. He has not grown and matured as he was intended to do. If he has been inhibited in his growth, he has been tampered with and treated unjustly as surely as though he had been deprived of food or air or sunlight or essential knowledge. If he has simply refused to grow, he is the person for whom we reserve, eminently, the title "immature."

All this should seem quite elementary and yet we know from the past that it has not always seemed so. New sources of information, new dimensions of understanding have at times been declared foreclosed by a church which appeared to have forgotten that it must learn before it can teach.

Neither Catholic nor Protestant Christianity entered grace-
fully into the new world revealed by the Copernican revolution which so profoundly changed man's thinking about
himself and about the universe that surrounded him. After
Copernicus, as a much later pope would acknowledge, man
found himself suddenly dethroned, no longer master of a
tidy, ordered world about which a whole universe had
revolved as its chosen centre. Instead, he discovered himself
at the periphery of a vastly different universe, a tiny creature
on a speck of cosmic dust in a sea of far greater worlds.
Possibly never before or since has he been required to alter
so radically his—in this instance taken most literally—
Weltanschauung: his "world-view," his way of understanding the totality of things. It is not to the credit of the church
that it so long hindered rather than helped him to do this,
by trying to convince him that he must remain in the now
defunct cosmos that had been taken for granted by biblical
writers and the preceding Christian centuries.

If the church has never reacted quite so disastrously to
subsequent intellectual revolutions, neither can it be claimed
that it has usually greeted them with marked enthusiasm.
Only with considerable footdragging has it now begun to
come to terms with the Darwinian revolution that lies in
the background of this book by Professor Haag. Far too
often theology, though proudly proclaimed a science, has
been thought of as a closed and completed canon of immu-
table knowledge. Formulations and constructs, including
biblical formulations and constructs, are by definition time-

conditioned and thus subject to the attrition of time. The temptation, however, was to canonize the formulation along with what it formulated. Those who yielded to this temptation could hardly be expected to fling wide the windows to the winds of change, which could only blow in "contemporary errors."

However, it would be unjust and self-serving to explain away all our failures as due to the intervention of an excessive and over-protective church discipline. This has played its part, but in turn it has been only a part of a far more pervasive reluctance of Christians to discard, even when these have been quite shattered, the worn-out earthen vessels in which they hold their treasures. The reason for this attitude is not hard to find, nor is the attitude confined to religious thinking. Very often there have been no new vessels close to hand, or seemed to be none, and men might be excused for preferring even the leakiest vessel to none at all. Every tradition encourages a conservatism which has its good as well as its bad effects. Patching up the old and the familiar is more congenial to most people than getting used to what is new and untried. There may come the time, of course, when even the most extensive patchwork will no longer do, but familiarity has a way of dulling one's awareness of that time.

As Professor Haag explains in this book, the theology common in the Catholic schools of our recent past tended to take the formulations of ecclesiastical magisterium as its starting point when dealing with a given doctrine of faith.

<u>In their light it interpreted the biblical passages that were</u>
<u>thought to be relevant</u>. Methodologically, the procedure left
much to be desired. The formulations are, of course, valu-
able and necessary to theology, embodying as they do the
church's periodic evaluations of its tradition under the
guidance of the Spirit. Nevertheless, as he reasonably ob-
serves, these conciliar decrees had certainly intended to say
no more than the Bible says: they were attempts to formulate biblical faith as the church then understood it. When,
in their letter, they were converted into criteria of how
the church must continue to understand biblical faith, the
true direction of theology was reversed. The church was
no longer permitted, by arriving at a deeper understanding
of the biblical word, to distinguish in the formulations of
the past between the perennially valid article of faith and
the contemporary presuppositions that had been its vehicle.
Theology now began to determine the word instead of being
determined by it. Indeed, in this topsy-turvydom of priori-
ties, the dogmatic theologian was encouraged to regard the
biblical exegete as the troubler of his sureties rather than as
the indispensable member of his resource personnel, and
the biblical word, from being his inspiration and direction,
became instead a source of bothersome "objections" to be
solved.

But exegetes, too, were not always immune to the same
mistake. Traditional in Catholic exegesis, from patristic
times down to the Second Vatican Council, has been the
principle of "the analogy of faith": that the word of God

is heard in the scripture only when it is interpreted in the same Spirit in which it was written, within the living tradition of the church. In equivalent terms this is also a Protestant principle. It is a principle that does not exclude but rather demands the application of every scientific and historical resource at our disposal for the correct interpretation of the biblical text; for only when we know as far as possible precisely what it meant to the community of faith in which it was proclaimed can we discern the message that it continues to have for faith today. Only then, through rigorous historical criticism, can we also be certain of what it does not say, of what are simply the human limitations of the Bible, words of men who lived and thought in times and terms other than our own.

But too often it has been too easy to abbreviate the exegetical task. We have been too timid to hear the voice of the Spirit speaking to the churches, demanding all the attendant risks of faith; we have preferred to cling to what was known and assured, or so we thought. Some Christian exegetes have so identified the written Bible with the word of God that the word ceased to be living: it became incapable of speaking other than in the language and with the cultural horizons of biblical man. This is biblicism, not biblical faith. It has not been, save in specific instances, a peculiarly Catholic vice. More often Catholics have fossilized the word in tradition itself, imprisoning it within another but no less bygone age, and imposing upon the Bible the presuppositions of their forebears. Instead of an "analogy of faith" we often looked for our analogues to an "age of faith." And this could lead from exegesis—"leading out" the meaning of the word—to what has been called eisegesis —"leading into" it the meaning we thought it ought to have.

All that we have been describing above has been happily, slowly but surely, disappearing in the church that we now know. The Second Vatican Council has been so often called in evidence to testify to the new working of the Spirit in the church of our times—it were perhaps better to say, to our renewed attendance to the working of the Spirit—that it may seem platitudinous to repeat the thought here. Nevertheless, the council has surely been one of the symptoms of such a reality, affecting and being affected by the biblical, liturgical and other theological "movements" that have so transformed the Catholic scene, bringing in the beginnings of a genuine reformation. The transformation will inevitably touch our teaching and preaching at every level. But the contemporary textbook and catechetical citations assembled in the first section of this book illustrate how much needs to be done in these areas, and quickly, if Christian doctrine is to retain the relevance we wish to ascribe to it for a modern age.

The Christian doctrine of original sin does have such a relevance, we believe, when it is disencumbered of the wholly irrelevant mythology that has been imposed upon it. It is the corollary of the primary affirmation of the biblical word: that man is saved, that he finds purpose and meaning in life and the explanation of his destiny not by his own efforts but by faith in God. He can be saved only by God's grace because he is a sinner, by his very condition as a human being one with a race of man whose total known history testifies to its sinful character, to its basic inability and consequent failure to save itself from the evil that its better instincts would have it avoid. Faith does not, of course, withdraw man from this sinful world or make him any less a human being. It does, however, in the Christian understanding, make him one with a potentially new human race whose head is Christ. In Jesus Christ have been revealed the way, the truth and the life of a God of love and peace. Faith does not separate man from his fellows, but constitutes him a witness for them to the Spirit of God's promise, to testify that man and his world need not be doomed to despair and frustration, that the power of sin can and will be broken.

Though many in the world find this biblical word unacceptable, it has, sometimes in quite different terms, certain correspondences with even a-theistic observations on man and life. It is a word that can be heard, and in Christian experience it has been confirmed.

Some present-day theologians prefer to deal with "original sin" simply as an existential fact of the human condition. It would seem, however, that in some sense we must think of a "beginning," whether or not temporally measurable, of man's historical condition as distinct from his creaturehood itself. The Bible is firm in its conviction that sin is the work of man, not God; even the Priestly writer of Genesis, who had no story of his own to tell about the origins of sin, knew that God made the heart of man good and that it was man who made it evil. But even though "original" may therefore remain a significant adjective in reference to the cause of the disorder of man's world, it can hardly be made the subject of an historical investigation. The only man known to the history that we know is sinful man; for any other history of man we have no sources.

That has been one cause of our difficulties. There was a time when it was thought we did have historical sources and that these were to be found in the Yahwistic story of man's fall in the book of Genesis. Loss of contact with the Bible's literary forms and with the cultural background that had shaped its message conspired to transform an etiological story—in form no different from the Yahwist's other etiological stories about the origins of music and shepherding and viniculture—into a history in the strict sense of a remembered past. We have long recognized the mistake that was then made, but we have not yet caught up with all the other mistakes that followed in its wake.

We speak nowadays of the need to "demythologize" the Bible, and there is a certain sense in which this term is apt. We know that heaven is not "up," that there are no "pillars" of the earth to be shaken, that the moon is not a "star" and that it does not "shine." We know how to hear the Bible when it uses this language; we are not bothered by its authors' cosmological presuppositions. But more often than not it is our own thinking about the Bible that must be demythologized. It is we rather than the Yahwist who have turned his story into a mythical picture of man's origins. We have done this in the face of an anthropology he never knew and despite all the evidence from Rusinga or the Olduvai Gorge. It was we who intruded theology into the province of biology, not Genesis, not St. Paul. If the Bible must be translated—its concepts, often, as well as its words—in order to speak to modern man, it must also be allowed to speak its own word and not one that has been imposed upon it in a past age which is no longer relevant to man as he knows himself to be. The Bible properly translated speaks as well to our times as it spoke to the times in which it was written: this is not just a pious aspiration, but a fact of some experience. It is not the Bible that modern man finds incomprehensible, but he can find quite incomprehensible the myth that we are capable of making of the Bible.

The work of biblical translation is an ongoing one for all of us who are committed to be hearers and doers of the word. In company with many other exegetes and theologians of today Professor Haag is one who is making it easier for us to hear the word with fewer of the distractions we once experienced. Every preacher of the gospel, every teacher of religion, every believer who would simply understand better what he believes will be grateful for this brief but thorough exegetical study.

BRUCE VAWTER, C.M.

I

The Question

The doctrine of original sin is not found in any of the writings of the Old Testament. It is certainly not in chapters one to three of Genesis. This ought to be recognized today, not only by Old Testament scholars, but also by dogmatic theologians. Nevertheless, it still seems impossible to discuss what is binding in the biblical creation story without bringing in original sin. If an exegesis of the paradise story takes proper account of literary form, this story's relation to original sin is immediately called into question. The problem becomes acute as soon as someone asks whether the traditional teaching on the preternatural gifts of the first man is supported by the stories in Genesis 1 to 3, and whether these stories teach, or at least imply, monogenism. The article "Monogenism" by Karl Rahner in the new edition of the *Lexikon für Theologie und Kirche*[1] shows to what extent such disparate things as scientific discussion, the biblical teaching of creation, and the Church's doctrine of original sin have become entangled in modern dogmatics. He says that monogenism must be demanded for dogmatic and theological reasons, even though it is, of course, not easy to show that the immediate sense of such scripture texts as Genesis 2:5 and 3:20 teach monogenism unequivocally and in necessarily explicit fashion.[2] But, he says, the scriptures throughout seem to take for granted that the solidarity of men, for weal or woe, is based on biological unity.

The final and decisive factor is the Church's, and the Bible's "teaching that original sin as a state of sin stemming from the deed of one man is a *'peccatum unum origine'*" (one sin in origin) and "that it is handed on, not by imitation, but by physical generation." For the Church's teaching (which, strangely enough, he considers prior to biblical teaching) he cites the "Decretum de peccato originali" of the council of Trent (D789f-DS 1512f) and the encyclical *Humani Generis* (D2328-DS 2897); for the biblical teaching he quotes Romans 5:12 and I Corinthians 15:21f. In this way the Genesis texts are not called on to support the dogma of original sin directly. They are involved, however, since both passages from Paul are considered authentic and binding interpretations of them. We must ask, though, to what extent they should be so considered.

The first section of this book will show how the dogma of original sin is presented today in theological studies and in catechetical instruction. In the second section, we will ask what Genesis 1 to 11 says about the irruption of sin into humanity. The third section will consider Paul's interpretation of the Genesis texts and its further development in tradition and the magisterium. The author hopes in this way to offer dogmatic theologians a welcome aid to a new interpretation of the usual doctrine of original sin—a new interpretation which they themselves have felt ever more urgently necessary.

II

Original Sin
in Present Church Teaching

SCHOLARLY DOGMATICS

It would be impossible to give here the history of the doctrine of original sin from Augustine to the present, and so we will touch on only a few important points. Every dogmatic work on original sin gives some information on it.[3] Our purpose here is to show, by means of representative examples from well-known German theological textbooks and American catechisms, how the doctrine of original sin is presented in scholarly theology as well as in catechetical instruction.

Katholische Dogmatik by M. Schmaus deserves to be listed first since it is the most widely used dogmatic manual in the German-speaking countries. Original sin is handled in volume two, part one, "God the Creator."[4] After the teaching on the creation and essence of man we find the doctrine about "the supernatural elevation of human nature in Adam and Eve" (pp. 441–472), and here "supernatural gifts in the strict sense" are distinguished from "preternatural gifts." As "preternatural gifts" Schmaus names:

(1) Bodily Immortality

The first man was promised bodily immortality. This is expressly defined as an article of faith by the Council of Trent (p. 452).

As a consequence of his nearness to God, man was to be to a certain extent free from the attacks of nothingness. Without the intermediary rupture which we call death, he would have been transferred to a life of enlightened understanding which we today can reach only through the transforming power of death (p. 453).

Scripture several times bears witness to the immortality of the body. Genesis tells us that God prescribed death as a punishment for disobedience. God said to the first man, "From every tree of the garden you may eat; but from the tree of the knowledge of good and evil you must not eat, for the day you eat of it you must die." (Cf. 3:19, 22.) (P. 454.)

(2) Freedom from Suffering

It is common theological teaching (*opinio communis*), although not unequivocally expressed by the magisterium,

that the first men were also free from suffering, the mark
of death. Suffering is a sign that we are subject to death;
it is the anticipation of death in life, a hint that the
bodily powers are becoming exhausted. Pain descended
upon man after he sinned, when God's curse struck him.
(Gen. 3:16ff.) (P. 457.)

The author meets the objection—which he apparently
expects—that the first man was free from suffering because
the laws of nature were different, with the following reflection:

Whoever lives by love, lives a life of intense and wakeful
gift of self. While he does this he does not feel something
which, otherwise, of itself, would cause him pain. Pain
does not consist in an abnormal objective change alone.
This becomes pain only when it is felt. When a man does
not notice the change that would cause pain, because his
attention is drawn to another quarter, he feels no pain
(p. 458).

(3) Freedom from Concupiscence

The first men were free from inordinate desires, so that
no inclination to evil arose in them; nor strife which might
have prevented their free decisions and put difficulties in
the way of their moral and religious actions.

There is no decisive doctrinal statement about what freedom they actually had from "inordinate" desires. This
thesis is, however, so closely connected to formal dogmas

that it approaches the certainty of an article of faith (*fidei proximum*) (p. 459).

Theology sees a scriptural proof of the teaching of freedom from inordinate desires in the Genesis story which relates that the two people were naked and were not ashamed. (Gen. 2:25 together with 3:7, 10.) (P. 456.)

(4) The Gift of Knowledge

Among the blessings of the painless state of the first two men the gift of knowledge is always named—meaning the gift of knowledge by which man was present to himself and to nature. Theologians are agreed (*opinio communis*) that the first men had great knowledge (p. 467).

(5) The World Was Different Before the First Sin.

Scripture bears witness that even the world outside of man, the realm of things and animals, was stricken in its mysterious depths by man's relation to God. The world outside of man was included in God's curse after the first sin (Gen. 3:16–19) and, because of man, became subject to corruption (Rom. 8:20). God's curse was not without effect. It brought into being a condition of the world which without sin did not exist and would not have existed. However, it is hard to say exactly what changes were caused by God's curse, because we cannot give an account of what a sinless world looked like. In any case, the astrophysical and geophysical conditions remained unchanged. . . . Before his sin man lived in peace and confident intercourse with God. He as yet knew no fear of God's revelation and of what was divine. The harmony between men and animals, and further, the harmony in the entire material and animal world accompanied the harmony between God and man. After sin the law: "The fear of you and the dread of you shall be upon every beast of the earth, and upon every bird of the air, upon everything that creeps upon the ground and all the fish of the sea; into your hands they are delivered" (Gen. 9:2) was in force (p. 468).

After the exposition of man's original state we find the teaching on the "original" sin (pp. 472–484) and on its consequences (pp. 485–498). At the beginning stands this thesis:

It is an article of faith: Adam and Eve in transgressing a divine law sinned gravely. This is stated by the Council of Trent, and further by the Synod of Carthage in the year 418 and by the Second Council of Orange in the year 529 (p. 472f.).

"Manner and Form of the Sin" are then presented in a close retelling of Genesis 3:1–7, in which, as in the section on the preternatural gifts of Adam and Eve, the literary form of the biblical story is ignored. The *"Consequences of the First Sin for Adam and Eve"* are described as follows:

The consequences of the turning away from God immediately went into effect. The Council of Trent enumerates these: loss of original holiness and justice, becoming subject to the anger and displeasure of God, to bodily death, to the power of the devil, and weakness of body and soul (p. 485).

In the development of this thesis according to Genesis 3:14–20, he concedes that it is in accordance with the opinion of St. Thomas to say, "that the text of Genesis does not give proof of a change in the structure of the snake" (p. 489), and likewise that one must say concerning the punishment of the woman "that the nature of woman has not been essentially changed by sin."

> Even without sin, pregnancy and giving birth would have involved changes in the organism that would of itself have caused pain . . . What was changed is the disposition and the sensitivity of the woman. As a consequence of sin, she is no longer able to integrate, in love, what objectively happens to her into the whole of her existence. She has become too weak for this.

Concerning the curse of Adam it must be said that the earth through sin experienced no change in its laws. Work is not a consequence of sin . . . Through sin, however, the relationship of man to the earth is changed in two ways: first, it must be said that the earth shares in some mysterious way in the diminution of human existence . . . Thus God's curse has primarily the effect that man, as a consequence of his selfishness and pride, uses the earth with covetousness, in his lust for power. In this way the earth is used contrary to its original purpose and so loses its possibility of offering man the unimpaired fertility he needs. As a consequence of the corruption brought about in nature through his own fault, man must now wring from the earth (by the sweat of his brow) that which without sin it would have been her only purpose to give him. . . .

After these considerations, it would be a one-sided interpretation to see the changes that God's punishment called forth only in man and not also in nature (p. 490f.).

Schmaus dedicates the next two chapters of his *Dogmatik* to "*Original Sin*"; the first, to the fact of its existence and its essence (pp. 498–515), the second to its consequences (pp. 515–528). In connection with the decrees of the Council of Trent, the existence and essence of original sin are thus formulated:

It is an article of faith, original sin exists; that is, a sin which from Adam was transmitted to all his posterity with the exception of the Most Blessed Virgin. Original sin is a true sin, although no sinful deed, but rather a condition of sinfulness. It is the death of the soul, and makes man an enemy of God, a son of wrath, unrighteous and godless. It dwells in every man by virtue of his descent from Adam (p. 499).

The *essence* of original sin is described by Schmaus in great detail thus:

Original sin is a condition in which man does not share
in the life and the glory of the triune God, in which he
stands under God's wrath and judgment. Original sin is a
lack of God-given righteousness.

This lack is inherent in man as a consequence of his being
descended from Adam. It is truly sin, but since it is no sinful deed, but rather a sinful situation, we can say that here
the word "sin" is being used analogously. Kinship of free
will also supports this analogous character; that is, original
sin is voluntary through the free will of Adam, the father
of the human race (p. 500).

Schmaus expresses himself as follows on the *existence* of
original sin:

Original sin really exists in each man from the moment he
comes into existence. The Old Testament speaks of the
general sinfulness of mankind, without ever mentioning
original sin explicitly . . . Christ himself mentions the
tendency of all men to sin, without, however, specifically
naming original sin. The fifth chapter of the Epistle to the
Romans offers a clear scriptural proof to which tradition
has always held (p. 506f.).

The "statement of the Magisterium" is based on this
chapter of Romans as Schmaus now sets forth. Schmaus
first presents the text of Romans 5: 8–21 in its entirety
in German. His commentary on it is of the greatest importance:

To confirm his readers' conviction in salvation through Christ, Paul compares the saving action of Christ to Adam's sin. As through Adam came damnation, so through Christ came salvation . . . Through Adam sin came into the world like a tyrannical power. Accompanying it was a fearful despot, death, who made his way to every single man . . . How had it come about that man was delivered up to sin, was in its power? Not through personal sin, but through the deed of Adam. All were involved and therefore all were sinners before God . . . And Paul too is convinced that all men have sinned. Death is to be traced back to Adam alone. All other men are subject to death, inasmuch as they share in Adam's sin . . . All men since Adam are sinners inasmuch as they share his sin, and all men have been delivered over to death because of this sinful state (pp. 508–510).

Finally, Schmaus is at variance with the idea of "some recent Catholic exegetes" who understand the phrase, "since all have sinned" (Romans 5:12) "not of the sharing in Adam's sin, but of the sinful deeds of Adam's posterity," and accordingly see in this phrase an effort on the part of Paul to stress the responsibility of each individual person.

According to this exegesis, verse 12 is no proof of the transmission of Adam's sin to all men. However, this interpretation holds that Chapter 5 of the Epistle to the Romans does indeed give proof of the existence of original sin in verse 19. It reads: "For just as by the disobedience of the one man the many were constituted sinners, so also by the obedience of the one many will be constituted just." The connection between the situation in which man finds himself and Adam's sinful deed is as close as that between Christ's work of redemption and the justification of men (p. 510).

In a last chapter Schmaus speaks about the transmission of original sin. He places at the beginning church teaching:

It is an article of faith: original sin is transmitted through natural generation. Each man is in the state of original sin as a consequence of his descent from Adam (p. 535).

This thesis is then developed:

Since Adam, as head of the human race, lost divine life and thus drew human nature into sin, each man is a sinner because he is a descendent of Adam and shares his human nature. The basis for the inheritance of sin is the unity of bodily life that binds all men to one another.

Of course, this inheritance must not be understood as a natural process in which original sin flows, so to speak, from parent to child. It means that each being which, through generation, becomes a member of the human race, as a consequence of his belonging to the humanity which stems from Adam, begins to exist without the divine supernatural life that God willed for him (p. 535f.).

This explanation is bolstered by a long quotation from Thomas Aquinas. Then Schmaus writes the significant sentence:

> The exposition of Saint Thomas leads us to conclude immediately that the unity of the human race, as monogenism would make it, is a necessary presupposition for the thesis that original sin is transmitted through physical reproduction (p. 537).

In his inaugural address as rector of Munich University entitled "Paradise" Schmaus again takes up the problem of the so-called "preternatural gifts."[5] While he maintains the same opinion as in his *Dogmatik* about man's freedom from pain before the Fall, he departs notably from his textbook on the questions of Knowledge and Immortality. Although in his *Dogmatik* the "theologians" are quite agreed on the great knowledge of the first two human beings, we read in "Paradise":[6]

> Scripture does not have the opinion that man in paradise— to use the language of science, the first man—had especially great knowledge. It assures us only that he was able to move instinctively, although not without danger, through the powerful and frightening world of things and animals. Genesis is also in agreement with that understanding of man according to which the first man lived in an intellectual twilight, and to such a measure that we might say (it is

absurd to say it but we can perhaps imagine such an absurdity) that if Adam had been suddenly set down in our scientific and technical world of today he would have gone crazy (p. 25).

Between 1962 and 1965 Schmaus revised his opinion on the immortality of the first man to an even greater extent than that about his knowledge (which in his *Dogmatik* had been given, however, as *communis opinio*). Immortality is given as an article of faith in the *Dogmatik*.[7] In "Paradise," however, Schmaus writes:

> Man, had he remained innocent, would have experienced death in a fashion quite different from the guilty man. Not death, but rather the experience of death, is for the sinful man not the same as for the guilty one. If one could decide to distinguish between death and dying, we could formulate the biblical teaching thus: Men would have been free from dying, but not from death, if they had not sinned— in other words, if they had maintained and would maintain communion with God (p. 26).*

Schmaus' pupil and successor, L. Scheffczyk, differs from his teacher and predecessor more in formulation than in content. In his article "Erbschuld," in the *Handbuch theo-*

---

*Editor's Note: Professor Schmaus has somewhat modified these views in *God and Revelation* (Sheed & Ward, N.Y.) to be published in 1969. The presentation of his position as given in the citations above still remains, however, as an excellent expression of the theology of original sin as it is presented in the majority of textbooks currently used in Catholic colleges and seminaries.

logischer Grundebegriffe,[8] he first states, concerning the biblical basis for the doctrine of original sin, that one finds little in the Old Testament to prove its existence. However:

> The conception of the general sinfulness of all men, the propensity to sin, and death as a consequence of an original sin, all factors in the fully developed teaching on original sin, may very well be seen as the point of departure for such a development (p. 295).

In Romans 5: 12ff., Paul, Scheffczyk says, on the one hand makes a connection between the common sinfulness of mankind and the deed of Adam, and this connection includes more than the loss of immortality. On the other hand, it cannot be said that a complete formulation of the concept of original sin is to be found in this passage. Here, Scheffczyk makes his own the formulation of O. Kuss (*Der Römerbrief* I, 231) that this passage, "could become the scriptural-theological basis of a teaching on original and inherited guilt." He says, however, that I Corinthians 15: 20–22 gives only a hint of the loss of immortality (p. 295f.).

Scheffczyk goes into the question of original sin more deeply in his thrilling article, "Die Erbschuld zwischen Naturalismus und Existentialismus," with the subtitle, "Can the dogma of Original Sin fit into modern thought?"[9] Section three, "The Reconciling Position of Catholic Theology," interests us above all. Here Scheffczyk first concedes that the idea of transmission of the first sin through hered ity has no exclusive right to express this particular revealed truth, because it looks onesidedly toward a natural or physical understanding which can scarcely be the decisive point in explaining a sin (p. 45).

"Hereditary sin" has not been successful in theology; it has been replaced by the expression "peccatum originale"; that is, "original sin," which expresses the idea that this sin came into being through man himself at his origin (p. 45f.). In fact, the natural events of descent and heredity cannot in themselves explain the transmission of sin; these natural factors play only a supporting role, dependent on God's decree (p. 46f.).

Since true causality on the part of the parents when original sin is transmitted is entirely lacking, it is advisable to look at the whole process from another point of view and to see it:

> as the entrance of a new human being into the already existing solidarity of mankind in evil, but it remains true that this entrance does not take place in external fashion only; it means rather that man's innermost self is affected by sin (p. 48).

The rejection of such a physical causality in the transmission of original sin makes more emphatically necessary, according to Scheffczyk, the recognition of a material-physical unity between Adam and mankind, "which should be understood, more exactly, as a unity based on blood relationship." According to Scheffczyk, we have here a "specifically Catholic teaching" (p. 48f.). He considers proved "that the universality of the loss of grace is guaranteed only within a closed community related by blood ties whose first ancestor alone has personally committed sin" (p. 51).

The unity of all mankind in the human nature of Christ demands, according to Scheffczyk, the greatest possible unity of the human race, that is, a bodily or biological unity resulting from a common parentage (p. 51f.). He acknowledges that he comes to this conclusion about redemption only because it seems appropriate. He next uses this conclusion, however, as an argument for original sin, and demands that original sin too must have taken place "in a community related by blood ties" (p. 52).

Therefore, Scheffczyk considers it necessary on theological grounds to hold the historicity of Adam as it is found in the Bible, and the more so, since this cannot be proved by exegesis but, at the same time, cannot be disproved. Scheffczyk does believe that everything that smacks of Utopia in man's original condition is to be excluded. Man's original condition is to be attributed, rather, to an inward grace-filled relationship with God. This, nevertheless, leaves room for the preternatural gifts:

The *donum immortalitatis* ("gift of immortality") would then mean the promise of a grace-filled change, excluding every fear of death, at the end of the earthly existence; the *donum impassibilitatis* ("gift of freedom from suffering") would mean the spiritual superiority of the soul filled by God with grace over the hostile powers of the external world (p. 53).

Finally, Scheffczyk takes up the question of the historicity of the sin of our first parents. He states that the historicity of redemption stands or falls with the historicity of original sin. This historicity must, as Scheffczyk explains, be taken for granted, according to Catholic thought, in conceiving the existence of a sinfulness characteristic of human nature. The personal character of this sinfulness, however, cannot be denied, because:

> Original sin has caused and still causes the majority of sins . . .   . . . When a man in the present sins, he completes the original decision of Adam, and gives original sin its historical realization. In this way the Sin of Nature takes on a personal character according to Catholic thought, as Paul expresses it in Romans 5:12 when he sees the sinfulness of all men as conditioned through the sin of Adam. Thus original sin reaches into the dimension of personal activity (p. 56).

Scheffczyk's most recent remarks on this subject can be read in his article, "Adam's Sűdenfall: die Erbschuld als Problem gläubigen Denkens Heute,"[10] in which Scheffczyk again attacks the problem of the "rather unanimous dissent of the modern world from church dogma," in order to "develop" a Catholic "restatement of the truth of original sin for human consciousness of the present day" (p. 769).

He says that "to reject the doctrine of original sin on scriptural grounds" is to "short-circuit the problem" (p. 763), although he doesn't say why. It cannot be said of the exegete who brings forward conscientiously tested questions and reflections arising from scriptural findings that he has already "made a dogmatic prejudgment on the impossibility of original sin" (p. 762). As "new insights," yielded by the "sharper eye" of today's theologian, Scheffczyk names the understanding of the threat of death in Genesis 2:17 which requires us to agree "that man in his original state of grace would *not*[11] have experienced death as the catastrophic consequence of sin in the manner that we do today" (p. 769). Even man in paradise, then, would really have experienced death in some specific fashion; and this is important for our question. The "restatement" of the dogma admits of this being said, according to Scheffczyk. Even more important, Scheffczyk, in this article, moves away from the oft-repeated "mechanical transmission of this fault" which burdens the individual with original sin and also from the image of inheritance. " 'Inheritance' is rather to be understood as an image of an inner indissoluble continuity, the unity of all men before God even in guilt" (p. 772f.).

In the symposium, *Theology Today*,[12] J. Feiner gives a summary of the teaching on "Man's Origin and Contemporary Anthropology" in present day theology (pp. 27–66) and takes the opportunity to declare his own stand on the question. He asks how far the modern scientific idea of the world forces theology to give up or revise its previous conceptions about the origin, original unity, and original situation of man. Feiner, anticipating the position of systematic theology, sketches as follows:

> The teaching office of the Church and Catholic theology hold fast to the *historical existence* of Adam. They do not do this because they are of the opinion that one should look for a strictly historical content in every detail of the biblical story of creation, nor from a desire to save as much as possible of the biblical concept of the world. They do so because the historical reality of Adam as the sole ancestor of all men and the historicity of the original state and of the Fall are presupposed by the Church's teaching, received from the revelation of the New Testament, regarding original sin and redemption (p. 31).

Although on the one hand, according to Feiner, the evolutionary world-view does not contradict the revealed truth "that at a particular time and particular place on earth, through a free action of God, the miracle of man's coming into being took place" (p. 244), he knows, on the other hand, that in the question of the original unity of humanity he is not free dogmatically:

> Holy Scripture and the Church speak of a unique individual man as the ancestor of all humanity . . . The origin of mankind (according to the teaching of the Church and Scripture) took place only once, and in a single couple,

through a creative intervention of God. All other men descend by generation from this first couple, and, by reason of this common origin, participate in the universal culpability of the human race which resulted from the historical fall of the first parents into sin (original sin) (p. 46).

Quoting the encyclical *Humani Generis,* Feiner makes his own the thesis of Karl Rahner that monogenism must be considered "theologically certain" (p. 252). Among the arguments that he gives for this, we find the "metaphysical principle of economy" (also used by Karl Rahner), according to which it would have been unreasonable for God to call other pairs of humans, capable of generation, into being, if a single pair were capable of reproducing sufficiently to form the whole human race (p. 255f.).[18] Feiner consequently sees only these alternatives:

On one hand there is the radical renunciation of the historical validity of the biblical and traditional assertions concerning Adam and the Fall. This necessarily involves a radical renunciation of the Church's doctrine of original sin and a denial of the doctrine of redemption. On the other hand, we can maintain the historical reality of a single ancestor, Adam, and of his Fall as the premise for the doctrines of original sin and redemption as they have always been understood by the Church (p. 57).

Although Feiner shows himself bound to tradition and the dogmatic basis of monogenism, his remarks on the grace of man's original state, and their effects in the physical realm, sound very untraditional in his article, "Urstand," in the *Lexikon für Theologie und Kirche* (X, col. 572–574). This article says that the durative significance of the "Old Testament aetiology" of Genesis 1–3 can be ascertained only through the "prospective aetiology" (eschata) given by the Christ-event.

> We may recognize the immanent dynamic of the grace of man's original state (which, because of the unity of the history of salvation, is to be conceived of as the grace of Christ) from the eschatological completion of humanity which in the resurrected Christ has already become present and manifest: this grace is directed to a thorough command of the entire spiritual-physical life of man in all its dimensions. The doctrine of the preternatural gifts of man's original condition describes the dynamic of divinizing grace according to its true content. Without original sin these gifts would have been uninterruptedly effective in man's earthly life, but of course, in a way corresponding to his life of pilgrimage. The immortality of the first man does not mean that the grace of his original condition would have kept his earthly life from ending; but this end would not have had the character of a painful death because of sin. It would have taken place in the uninterrupted submission of man to the gracious God.[14]

These thoughts are quite in line with Feiner's claim in the preamble of his article:

The doctrine of man's original condition (is) to be reflected upon anew in the light of today's knowledge of the literary forms in the Bible and of earlier epochs' ways of thinking (col. 572).

In the dogmatic section of the article, "Erbsünde," in the *Lexikon für Theologie und Kirche* (III, col. 965–973), J. Auer tries with carefully shaded formulations to confront the traditional doctrine of original sin with more recent queries. He sees in Romans 5:12–19 the explanation, given with scriptural authenticity, of what the Old Testament says about man's sinfulness. Auer seems to make his own the predominant conception of counter-reformation theology on the essence of original sin, according to which original sin consists in a lack of sanctifying grace; it includes, however, a negative factor; it causes man to be autocratic and lonely. Original sin, according to this definition, is for Auer a "guilty state" (col. 967), "truly guilty" insofar as it is "the lack of *justitia et sanctitas originalis* (original justice and holiness) which were given by God and are therefore owed to him (col. 970), and thus it is worthy of 'destruction'" (col. 971). According to Auer, we should not speak of the "inheritance" of original sin in a strict sense. He puts the word "inheritance" in quotation marks. It lies in the "natural relationship to Adam through parentage," which is why *Humani Generis* demands monogenism (col. 971). Auer speaks with great reserve on the consequences of original sin for earthly life. "How far into the deeper personal realm of man the effects of original sin reach, so that even the baptized person is likely to be autocratic and lonely and can overcome temptation only by the help of God's ever-renewed grace, must be further explained" (col. 971).

CATECHETICS

Since the Council of Trent there has been very little change in catechetical handbooks, but in the United States, thanks mostly to the efforts of teaching sisters, catechisms have recently begun to change.

There is great variation in style, rather less in content, among the many catechisms now in use, with the *Baltimore Catechism* and the *Priory Press Series* at the one end of the scale, and such accomplishments as Sister M. Elizabeth and Sister M. Johnice's *Bible, Life and Worship Series* at the other. An attempt has been made in the latter, as well as in many newly published series, to return to the biblical teaching; in spite of this the basic teaching of the Tridentine Catechism on original sin is repeated in nearly every volume and at every age level. The only exception is *The Dutch Catechism,* recently published in English, whose presentation of scripture is very reliable.

The *Baltimore Catechism*,[15] with which nearly all but the youngest Catholics have long been very familiar, takes the form of questions and answers, among which the following interest us:

52. What was the chief gift bestowed on Adam and Eve by God?

The chief gift bestowed on Adam and Eve by God was sanctifying grace, which made them children of God and gave them the right to heaven.

53. What other gifts were bestowed on Adam and Eve by God?

The other gifts bestowed on Adam and Eve by God were happiness in the Garden of Paradise, great knowledge, control of the passions by reason, and freedom from suffering and death.

56. What happened to Adam and Eve on account of their sin?

On account of their sin Adam and Eve lost sanctifying grace, the right to heaven, and their special gifts; they became subject to death, to suffering, and to a strong inclination to evil, and they were driven from the Garden of Paradise.

In explanation: "The loss of sanctifying grace and the special gifts marked the beginning of that conflict between man's lower powers and his reason."

57. What has happened to us on account of the sin of Adam?

On account of the sin of Adam, we, his descendants, come into the world deprived of sanctifying grace and inherit his punishment, as we would have inherited his gifts had he been obedient to God . . .

59. Why is this sin called original?

This sin is called original because it comes down to us through our origin, or descent, from Adam.

60. What are the chief punishments of Adam which we inherit through Original Sin?

The chief punishments of Adam which we inherit through Original Sin are death, suffering, ignorance, and a strong inclination to sin.

In explanation:

(a) The fact of Original Sin explains why man is so often tempted to evil and why he so easily turns from God.

(b) Because of the ignorance resulting from Original Sin, the mind of man has difficulty in knowing many necessary truths, easily falls into error, and is more inclined to consider temporal than eternal things.

(c) The penalties of Original Sin—death, suffering, ignorance and a strong inclination to sin—remain after Baptism, even though Original Sin is taken away.

After the questions and answers, a more general explanation of some of the teachings on original sin is offered in the catechism:

God bestowed on Adam and Eve wonderful privileges, they dwelt in a beautiful garden; they were free from inordinate inclinations to sin; they were preserved from suffering, they were destined never to die, but after a space of time on earth, to be taken body and soul into heaven. Above all, they were endowed with the precious gift of sanctifying grace, that made them the beloved children of God.

It was God's plan that these privileges should be transmitted from Adam to all his descendants. However, he made this dependent on the faithfulness of Adam in obeying his command not to eat the fruit of a particular tree. Adam disobeyed; and hence lost these precious gifts for himself and for all his descendants. Eve also sinned and lost the privileges for herself . . .

The entire human race is descended from Adam and Eve; hence, we all enter the world deprived of the gifts we should have had if Adam had not sinned. The deprivation of sanctifying grace, called Original Sin, brings with it the necessity of submitting to suffering and to death.

The *Priory Press Series,* used in many undergraduate "theology" courses, offers the college student the basic Tridentine teaching in a neoscholastic framework, with a fundamentalist interpretation of scripture. From this series we quote the following:

On the creation of man:

Because of man's pre-eminence, his creation calls for a special intervention on the part of God. The sacred author clearly indicates this in his account: expressing the solemnity and significance of the event. God, as it were, previously takes counsel with himself: "Let us make man to our image and likeness."[16]

The author does not discuss the question of monogenism at all. But it is certainly taken for granted in his unquestioning belief in a historical Adam and Eve.

On the perfection of Adam's intellect:

The intellect of the first man was highly endowed with knowledge, both natural and supernatural . . .

His supernatural knowledge of God came from the virtue of faith; his natural knowledge of God from infused ideas and from the consideration of the sensible and intelligible effects of the divine causality. Adam's contemplation of the immaterial effects of God (the order and harmony of the universe, for example) was not impeded by the distractions caused by sensible and exterior things. The lower powers of his soul were in complete subjection to the higher powers, so that his contemplation of God was clear and steadfast, unhindered by preoccupation with exterior things.

The first man possessed all the natural knowledge that the intellect can know by its own power . . . Adam had his natural knowledge from the beginning through infused ideas.

Since man was elevated to the supernatural order, Adam received also the knowledge of all supernatural truths necessary to direct himself and others to their supernatural end. These extraordinary gifts of natural and supernatural knowledge were given to Adam not as an individual, but as the head and the teacher of the human race . . .

Adam could not have made mistakes nor could he have been deceived. His reason had perfect control over his other faculties, so that he could not have been impelled by passion, forgetfulness, inconsideration, or any of the other things that cause error in judgment and reasoning.[17]

On the perfection of Adam's will:

The first man was endowed with sanctifying grace and elevated to the supernatural order. This is a defined doctrine of faith . . .

Adam's original perfection, which this grace conferred, consisted in a perfect, ordered harmony; it comprised three things: (1) the perfect subjection of his body to his soul; (2) the perfect subordination of the lower powers of his soul to his reason; and (3) the perfect submission of his reason to God . . .

Due to the perfection of his state, . . . he had none of the emotions which are concerned with evil, such as fear, sadness, etc. In the state of innocence there was no such thing as sensible evil; evil was neither present nor imminent . . . Adam had complete control over his passions, and they could not be exercised contrary to the judgment of his reason.

Together with grace, Adam had all the theological and moral virtues. Some of the moral virtues, however, he had only by way of habit, for their exercise was not called for in the state of innocence. Thus, before he sinned, he could not exercise the virtue of penance; and since there was no unhappiness in paradise, he could not perform works of the virtue of mercy.[18]

On the immortality of Adam:

Our first parents, in the state of original justice were immortal; if they had not sinned they would never have had to die. Holy Scripture testifies that death was the result of sin . . .

The incorruptibility of Adam's body was a preternatural gift bestowed by God.[19]

Other preternatural gifts:

Our first parents enjoyed another preternatural gift, that of impassibility, or freedom from suffering. This was an effect of immortality, for suffering is a prelude to death. Adam was able to preserve himself from harm "partly through his own use of reason, by which he was able to avoid anything harmful; partly through divine providence, which so protected him that no harm would come upon him unexpectedly . . ."

If Adam had not sinned, these preternatural gifts and the supernatural gift of grace would have been transmitted to his descendants . . .

Physically, children born in the state of innocence would have been perfectly healthy . . .

Children born before the sin of Adam would have been born in a state of original justice, with that perfect subjection of body to soul, of the lower appetites to reason, and of reason to God. As soon as the soul was created and infused into the body by God, it would have had the gift of sanctifying grace . . .

They would have had clear insight, retentive memory, and sound judgment, without the impediments of ill health or the inordinate attractions of the senses.[20]

In summary:

Our first parents never existed in a state of pure nature, but from their creation were elevated to the supernatural order. They were endowed with the supernatural gifts of sanctifying grace, the theological and moral virtues, and the gifts of the Holy Ghost, along with the preternatural gifts of integrity, immortality and impassibility.

As head of the human race, Adam possessed the perfection of natural knowledge through ideas infused by God . . .

If Adam had not sinned, his children would have been born with all the supernatural and preternatural gifts.[21]

Together, the *Baltimore Catechism* and the *Priory Press Series* present the basic material to which all other American catechisms adhere. However, in recent years we have had many rather interesting variations of this theme.

Perhaps the most important catechism internationally is the well-known *German Catechism* which underwent some twenty-two translations in its first five years. It appeared in the United States in a three-volume edition under the title, *A Catholic Catechism,* also published in a one volume paperback condensation entitled *The Living Faith,* and intended for adults. Its teaching on creation and original sin is as follows:

GOD CREATED MEN

God made the body of man out of earthly materials. He created the soul out of nothing. Through it he gave life to the body. The first human beings were Adam and Eve; all men are descended from this original pair who are thus called our "first parents". . .

God made men in his love to see him and to live eternally with him; therefore God gave them a share in his own inmost life. This great gift, which was in no way earned, we call the life of grace, or sanctifying grace. By this gift of life the first men became children of God and like God in a special way.

God also gave to our first parents some other wonderful gifts. They were allowed to live in Paradise (which means "pleasant place") where they were especially close to God. He illumined their understanding with a special light and strengthened their will with special power. Their longings and their strivings were all towards what was good. The first human beings were free from the inclination to do evil and lived happily in God's presence. Work was not tiresome for them; they were free from suffering, sickness, and all evil, and they were to be preserved from death. All these gifts we call the special gifts of Paradise. The graces which God gave to our first parents were to have been inherited by all men. All men were to receive from Adam, along with their bodily life, the life of grace and the special gifts which Adam had had in Paradise. All these gifts together we call original grace.

35. What was the most precious gift which God gave to the first of mankind?

The most precious gift which God gave to the first of mankind was the gift of the life of grace.

36. What were men supposed to inherit from Adam besides the life of their bodies?

Besides their bodily life, all men were to inherit from Adam the life of grace and the special gifts of Paradise.[22]

OUR FIRST PARENTS COMMITTED SIN

In the hour of their trial our first parents did not listen to God, but rather followed the devil and ate of the fruit; they wanted to be as God was. Adam and Eve knew clearly that they were disobeying God's command, and yet they did so of their own free wills. They sinned seriously against God. This sin of Adam and Eve we call the first sin. Their guilt passed on to us we call Original Sin.

By this sin committed in Paradise our first parents ceased to be the children of God; they lost the life of grace and were no longer fit to enter heaven. That was the worst result of their sin. By their sin they also lost the special gifts of Paradise. They might no longer live in special nearness to God, and had to leave Paradise. Their intelligence was darkened and their power of will was made weaker; they now had an inclination towards evil. They had many things to suffer, and had to earn daily food with much wearisome labor; and at the end of it all they had to die. Through the sin of our first parents the devil won power over mankind . . .

38. What did our first parents lose by Original Sin?

Through Original Sin, our first parents lost the life of grace and the special gifts of their stay in Paradise.

THE RESULTS OF ORIGINAL SIN
FOR ALL MEN

Through one man sin entered into the world and through sin death, and thus death has passed unto all men because all have sinned.[23] Because Adam, who was the head of all mankind, committed sin, the guilt of his sin has been inherited by all his descendants. This is called Original

Sin, or the "heritage of guilt." Because of Adam's sin we are born without the life of grace which, according to God's plan, we were to inherit from Adam. Only God's mother remained free of the heritage of guilt by a special privilege of grace.

In addition, the evil results of the sin of Adam have descended on all men; that is why we have an inclination to sin, which is called concupiscence. This shows itself in an unreasonable desire for the things of this world; for example, pleasure, possessions, honor, and fame. Moreover, men have to endure many troubles and sufferings and must finally die. Through Original Sin the devil obtained power over the world . . .

39. What misfortune did Adam's sin bring upon all mankind?

All men have inherited the guilt of Adam's sin and its evil consequences.

40. What does the heritage of guilt consist of?

The heritage of guilt consists of this: that because of Adam's sin we come into the world without the life of grace which, according to God's plan, we should have inherited from Adam.[24]

Among the new experiments in catechisms, the Regnery Series, *To Live is Christ,* attempts to take a teenager's point of view in exhorting high school students to good behavior.

The doctrinal content is very small, though often accompanied with liberal quotations from scripture. It has the following to say about original sin:

> Have you ever felt . . . like the real you, the better you, is anxious to make its appearance but is somehow trapped inside and can't get free?

> If so, you are not the only person who feels this way. All of us do. We cannot become the person we want to be unless we fight for it. This is a fight we're born with. We are all born with built-in obstacles, such as ignorance, laziness, selfishness. *This state of being born with built-in obtsacles to our own development is what we Catholics call Original Sin.*

> Because of the weaknesses we are born with, we often let other people keep us from being ourselves . . .

> Because of Original Sin, and the bad influence other people sometimes have on us, it is impossible to become the person God wants us to be without his help.[25]

Here it may be noted that the most widely used catechisms written for grade school children reflected for a long time the then prevalent limited understanding of the scriptural texts. Among these catechisms, the first *On Our Way Series,* written between 1957–1962, arranged the presentation of original sin according to an eight-year program. Under existing pressures this program relied on questions and answers from the *Baltimore Catechism.*

It also must be noted that this series is being replaced by the new *On Our Way Series, Vatican II Edition*,[26] in which the treatment of original sin reflects the current common interpretation of Holy Scripture. Sin is presented from a more existential point of view, and the story of Adam and Eve is not mentioned until sixth grade.

The following excerpts from the first *On Our Way Series* (1957–1962) reflect a way of teaching which still persists among American Catholics.

Grade 1:

> God made Adam and Eve. They were the first man and woman. God loved Adam and Eve in a very special way. He gave them a share in his own life and love. God made Adam and Eve to be his own children. They had the right to go to heaven . . .
>
> What special gift did God give Adam and Eve?
>
> God gave Adam and Eve the special gift of his own life and love.

A SAD STORY
Adam and Eve disobeyed God

> Adam and Eve did not obey God. They sinned. God was not pleased with them. God is all-just. He punished Adam and Eve for their sin. He put them out of the beautiful garden. They had to suffer. They had to die one day. Their worst punishment was the loss of God's life in them. They

were no longer children of God. They lost the right to go to heaven for us too. They lost for us the gift of God's life. We all have to suffer and to die one day.[27]

Grade 2:

Adam and Eve disobeyed God's command. They committed sin. It was a very big sin. God was very much displeased with them. Adam and Eve were punished. Heaven was closed to them and to their children. The sin of Adam is passed on to us . . .

24. Who committed the first sin on earth?

Our first parents, Adam and Eve, committed the first sin on earth.

25. Is this sin passed on to us from Adam?

Yes, this sin is passed on to us from Adam.

I was born with the stain of Adam's sin. This sin in us is called Original Sin. I was not a child of God. I had no right to heaven. But when I was baptized . . . baptism washed away the stain of sin.

41. What did Baptism do for you?

Baptism washed away Original Sin from my soul and made it rich in the grace of God.[28]

Grade 3:

God made Adam and Eve his children. He gave them a share in his own life. God wanted them to share his happiness in heaven. But Adam and Eve offended God. They lost his grace by committing sin. Heaven was closed to them and all their children.

The sin of Adam and Eve brought death and pain into the world.[29]

Grade 5:

According to the great plan of God, man was to share his life, happiness, and glory. When God created our first parents, he gave them great gifts of body and soul. These gifts were to pass from Adam and Eve to us, their children. The greatest gift of God was sanctifying grace, a share in his own life. Through sanctifying grace Adam and Eve would be able to enjoy God forever in heaven after their test on earth.

Adam and Eve turned away from God's plan. They were ungrateful to God. By their sin they lost the gift of grace both for themselves and for us, their children. They no longer had the right to enjoy God forever in heaven.[30]

Grade 6:

10. What was the most precious gift God gave to our first parents?

The most precious gift God gave to our first parents was a share in his divine life, sanctifying grace, which made them his children and heirs of heaven.

11. What are some other gifts which God gave to our first parents?

God gave our first parents the gifts of freedom from sickness, suffering, and death, and freedom from evil desires.

God's command to our first parents was a very serious and solemn one. Their loving and free obedience would win for them eternal happiness in heaven. Their disobedience would be punished with death and the loss of divine life . . .

God's command had been broken, and his love had been rejected. His justice now demanded that Adam and Eve be punished for their sin . . .

God revealed the punishment that Adam and Eve and all their descendants would suffer and die . . .

Because of their sin, Adam and Eve were exposed to evil desires, sickness, suffering, and death. However, their greatest punishment was the loss of God's friendship and the gift of his divine life, sanctifying grace. Adam and Eve were no longer God's children. They no longer had the right to be happy with him in heaven. These results of Original Sin are inherited by the human race.

14. What happened to our first parents because of their sin?

Because of their sin, our first parents lost the gift of divine life, sanctifying grace. They were also exposed to evil desires, sickness, suffering and death.[31]

Grade 7:

God gave our first parents a body and an immortal soul, with the powers to think and choose. Above all, he gave them a share in his own divine life . . .

Adam and Eve were very happy. They were closely united with their heavenly father in a pleasant and holy friendship. They formed the first worshiping community of God's children on earth.

In time, however, our first parents ruined their beautiful relationship with God. When God tested their love, they willfully disobeyed. They lost divine life for themselves and their descendants.[32]

Grade 8:

The first Adam received life and lost it for all. The New Adam conquered death and lives for us all.

Death is a punishment for sin, "The wages of sin is death, but the gift of God is life everlasting in Christ Jesus our Lord." We know that our first parents, Adam and Eve, did not persevere in obedience. They chose to say "No" to God. They failed their test. They sinned. Death then came into the world as a punishment for sin. "Therefore as through one man sin entered the world and through sin death, and thus death has passed unto all men because all have sinned."[33] [34]

The Bible, Life, and Worship Series,[35] written by Sister M. Johnice and Sister M. Elizabeth, reduces the question-answer format to a brief summary at the end of large sections of text. Its outstanding illustrations deserve mention. It presents many of the biblical stories and themes but does not trust the Bible to speak for itself. Doctrinally, the series' strongest point, particularly in reference to original sin, is that it avoids much which is extreme and distasteful. But what it does say gives us no new understanding of original sin. At this writing the series was not yet completed, and only the first four volumes were examined.

In the text for Grade One, the student is informed that, through their sin, Adam and Eve lost their state of complete happiness, as well as grace ("the gift of God's kind of life"). Further, Adam and Eve, through their disobedience, lost these gifts "for us, too."

This theme is taken up again in the text for Grade Two, but here new notes are added. Adam brought the darkness of sin and death into the world; as a result of his fall, each of us is born without the life of grace, i.e., we are born with original sin. Jesus' suffering and death were to make up for our sins, and win for us the life of grace lost by the sin of Adam.

The authors of the *Bible, Life and Worship Series* have already revised their treatment of original sin in the Confraternity Edition, and are revising the Parochial School Edition. The earlier editions have been referred to here merely to illustrate how the "doctrine" of original sin, widely taught on every level, has been quite separated from its possible scriptural base in Genesis.

THE DUTCH CATECHISM

The publication of an English translation of the official Dutch Catechism[36] brings us for the first time a catechism that generally remains faithful to the scriptural teaching about original sin, and may for that reason act as a guide to all future American catechisms. It is quoted here extensively.

Redemption co-extensive with sin. Sin is never seen in a pure state, so to speak, in the world. Humanity has never existed except as the race of men into which Jesus was to come or has come. Even in the most barbarous society of the past or of the present, man was always a fellow-man of Jesus, the Son of God. A newly-born child, as yet unbaptized, has been ushered into a world where redemption is at work. From the very beginning, he is a fellow-man of Christ and called to his friendship. And as regards adults— no matter how morally bankrupt a life may be, no matter how much evil a man permits himself, no one is proscribed, no one is excluded from the call of the good God (p. 259).

Universal Guilt. But this does not mean that one cannot suddenly experience in one's own life and in that of the world around a mysterious sense of guilt. We are oppressed by the inevitability of wars which break out like ulcers, though nearly everybody is against them; by the natural arrogance of capitalism and colonialism; by the poisoning of the atmosphere by racial and class hatred. Six million men perished in gas-chambers, on the highly civilized continent of Europe.

Our selfish incapacity to love one another, our failure to change our life and thinking is part and parcel of all this. We too do harm to men. We play our part in the great evil of the world. Our hands are not clean. "So the whole world may be held accountable to God" (Rom. 3:19) (p. 260).

The editors then consider the scriptural problems:

The Message of Genesis 1–11. From its own bitter experience, the faith of Israel had come to recognize the constancy of this element in human history. Hence the primeval history recounts a Fall four times over: the eating of the forbidden fruit, the murder of a brother, the corruption of Noah's contemporaries and the building of the tower of Babel (pp. 261–262).

The Message of Romans ch. 5. In the New Testament there is better comprehension of the fact that God's message contains these elements. Paul in particular, in the fifth chapter of the Epistle to the Romans, brings it out in its profundity. At first sight it seems that his intention is to stress the fact that it was through one man that sin came into the world. But the repetition of the word "one," occasioned by the view of the world history as it existed in Paul's time, is only part of the literary dress, not the message. What this difficult passage teaches is that though sin and death ruled over mankind, grace and eternal life, the restoration, has come in greater abundance through Jesus (p. 262).

The Fall a message about man, not about the beginning. Of all these texts, the biblical story of the Fall is the one which is most deeply impressed on our minds. But we must remember that, as we have said, the following chapters contain the same message. It is no doubt particularly striking in the story of Adam and Eve. The whole glory and misery of human life are here summed up in a few short and graphic words. This most moving text of Scripture can never be replaced as a summary of how man stands before God. But it can and must be replaced as a description of the beginning of mankind. We shall now dwell for a moment on the question of what we are to think of the beginnings of sin.

In earlier times, indeed, until recently, our picture of the world was primarily static, or stable. Things persisted the way they first existed. If one wanted to say something about the basic elements of existence, one showed how things were at the beginning. The explanation lay there.

The explanation of the very existence of things was that God had created them. He was spoken of like a carpenter who had made something and left it there.

The existence of sin was explained primarily by the fact that man had sinned.

But now our picture of the world has changed. We can see further into the distant past. It helps us to see that the world is involved in an upward movement, in a process of growth, one way or another. Our view of the world is no longer static but dynamic. This means that the authentic enlightenment is to be sought not in the beginning but in the course of things and their culmination. It is better to say, God creates, than to say, God created. To put it in very human terms: if he were to withdraw his creative hands from us for an instant, there would be nothing there. God is not a carpenter who can go away. The whole universe exists in God and depends on God. Creation grows in his hands. The whole course of history is his work, and it is only the whole that will explain it all and show that "everything was very good." (Gen. 1:31.)

Hence the beginning is less important to us than it was in earlier days. This is also true of sin. The meaning of the first sin needs to be pondered deeply. It is not of supreme importance that man sinned and was corrupted. He sins and becomes corrupt. The sin of Adam and Eve is closer than we imagine. It is in our own selves.

The Entry of Sin. Nonetheless, with regard to sin in particular, we cannot but continue to ask how it began. We expect some sure answer from the beginnings, which will explain how this incredible mistake crept into God's work. No matter how slow and gradual we imagine the beginnings to have been, sin must have had a beginning at one time or another. The answer will be, as it was when a different picture of the world obtained, that sin has to do with human freedom. Freedom grew in man and hence sin. But does not this seem to suggest that sin was inevitable?—All that we can say is that sin is committed with a certain freedom—otherwise it would not be sin—and freedom means that one could have done otherwise. But this does not necessarily mean that all sins in general could have been avoided. That any particular sin is committed is not inevitable, but that evil takes place is, perhaps, inevitable in practice. We do not know. Our mind is always impotent when it comes to understanding the beginning of evil—even in our own lives. When we have really sinned, we know deep within us that we have done so. We know we are guilty, and yet we ask ourselves in astonishment—how could I have done such a thing? And indeed evil is not comprehensible. It is the great absurdity, the great irrelevancy. And hence its origin in world history remains incomprehensible.

But evil exists, and against God's will. Nonetheless, he has power, as we believe, to bring greater good out of evil (pp. 262–264).

The common evil. In a certain sense, Scripture is a history of sin. The stories of Gen. 1–11 are followed by the history of the chosen people. Again and again it is seen to be obstinate, apostate, "adulterous"—a faithless spouse (Hos. 1–3). Here it should be noted that the people *as a whole* is described as sinful. Later parts of the Old Testament stress, no doubt, the responsibility of the individual. But there is still the feeling that sin is a matter of collective responsibility.

Jesus too points to a certain common responsibility in sin when he says, for instance, to the Pharisees that they commit their crimes (so) "that upon you may come all the righteous blood shed on earth." (Mt. 23:35.) And when we read in John, "Behold, the Lamb of God, who takes away the sin of the world" (Jn. 1:29), we see that the evil committed by man is taken to be one great sinfulness. It is the sin, not the sins, that is taken away (p. 265).

Reluctance in face of Christ. This solidarity in guilt is something which is never fully perspicuous to man. Evil is always obscure. Even in former times, theologians did not claim to have understood it fully. They looked to "human nature" which was propagated by bodily generation since sinful Adam. But this explanation of the collectivity or "oneness" of sin is not something which has been directly revealed. It is not part of the direct intention of revelation (what is *per se* revealed). The unity of the human race, according to Scripture, is not based on propagation ("Greek, barbarian or Jew") but on the call by the one Father. The oneness of sin is to be sought on the same level, though here in man's refusal. It reaches us, not merely by way of generation, but from all sides, along the ways in which men have contact with one another. The sin which stains others was not only committed by an Adam at the beginning of man's story, but by "Adam," man, every man. It is "the sin of the world." It includes my sins. I am not an innocent lamb which is corrupted by others. I help in the work of corruption (p. 266).

At the time of Augustine, c.400, this general sinfulness which we know both from Scripture and experience was given the name of *peccatum originale,* original sin. The Greek Fathers of the Church used the word "death," the death of the soul. The stress laid on the fact that this inheritance of original sin came by way of generation from one's parents led to much discussion of original sin in infants. But when we take a more complete view of the contamination, and see it as coming from all mankind, the stress is rather laid on adult man. Original sin is the sin of mankind as a whole (including myself) in so far as it affects every man. In every personal sin, the original sin of man is basically present and active and contributory.

We must always remember that this "original sin" is not a sin in the ordinary sense of the word. It may be said that it only takes on concrete form in our personal sins. Hence no one is condemned for original sin "alone," but only for the personal decisions by which he ratified original sin, so to speak, and stood over it. (So too baptism is also initiation into a life-long struggle against personal sin.) (Pp. 266–267.)

Was the world changed by original sin? Thomas Aquinas said long ago that to believe that wild beasts were then tame was a sign of "a feeble mind"—though this opinion could still be heard in our schooldays. There is no reason which compels us to believe that creation was different before man sinned. There may always have been thorns and thistles.

And as regards man himself, we need not imagine that he once existed in a state of paradisiac perfection and immortality. We have seen what the story of paradise and the fall intended to convey: the purpose of God, as realized in the whole, and above all in the end. We really know nothing of the actual beginnings. The imagery of the curse under which man was banished from paradise (Gen. 3:16-19)—thorns and thistles, birth-pangs, the sweat of the brow and the tragic conflicts of marriage—simply affirms that these things are not part of God's most profound and ultimate intention. It also says that sin is connected with such things.

Sin makes the world less good. Where sloth reigns, the fields grow thistles and the dykes collapse. Where there is hatred, a city is brought down in ruins. But gravest of all: a humanity in sin finds the world a heavy weight to bear. Everything looks darker to those who are inwardly ill at ease. The thistles and thorns are within man himself.

Sin and death, forgiveness and life. There is a very special and mysterious connection in our minds between sin and death. Holy Scripture sometimes expresses this by saying that through sin death came into the world. But since the beginnings are obscure to us, the beginning of biological death is also obscure. What we de see, when we look at the course of the history of salvation, is that along with sin death lost its sting. The resurrection of Jesus proclaims not merely forgiveness but eternal life. The consummation of human history will bring with it, as well as the complete conquest of sin, the complete conquest of death. Every member of the human race who allows himself to be saved from sin, will hear what the criminal heard from the lips of Jesus: "Today you will be with me in Paradise" (pp. 269–270).

The editors of the *Dutch Catechism* conclude their interpretation of original sin and their catechism with:

> We shall reassure our hearts before him
> whenever our hearts condemn us;
> *For God is Greater than Our Heart* (p. 502).

SUMMARY

Our review of the presentation of the doctrine of original sin in dogmatics and in catechesis of the present has shown that their ways of thought are unmistakably stamped by the heritage of a thousand-year-old theological tradition which, as we shall see, began with Augustine and concluded, for the present, with the Council of Trent. It is essential to this tradition of original sin that the sin of Adam, understood as an individual person, was transmitted to every member of the human race by way of a physical as well as a moral blood relationship, and that every member of the human race, even before any personal sinful deed, is by nature a sinner. To describe this doctrine the term "inherited sin" has been seen as appropriate. The "inheritance" thus expressed also covers, in the usual teaching, certain preternatural gifts which Adam had before his sin, but which he lost through sin, thereby robbing his descendants of them.

Nevertheless, in this review we may note a change of emphasis. Here and there the term "original guilt" is preferred to original sin because the concept of sin really involves the idea of a personal sinful act which in "original sin" is not present. Whether the word "guilt" does not increase the burden laid on the unparticipating descendant of Adam is another question. And it is recognized, at least theoretically, although not completely, that the idea of inheritance ought better to be avoided because it lends support to a biological-mechanical view of the transmission of this sin, whereas this actually lies in an inner solidarity of all men with their ancestor. Nevertheless, a monogenetic origin of mankind is generally demanded although dogmatic theologians have registered certain reservations[37] precisely on this point (in spite of *Humani Generis*). The preternatural gifts of man before the Fall have been questioned: so much, in fact, that previously held "dogmas" have ceased to be dogmas, to the great dismay of those who believe in the immutability of dogmas. Indeed, we find here not merely interpretation but correction of previous teaching.

Dogmatic theologians are very uncertain about how to define the essence of original sin. This is partly because, as we shall see, the Council of Trent did not define it. The same is true of the explanation of *how* original sin was transmitted to Adam's posterity.[38] Many contradictions are involved in the tendency to explain original sin as a lack of sanctifying grace, a lack to which guilt is ascribed and which in consequence must not only be removed, but destroyed. Dogmatic theologians are now demanding a new orientation, a new interpretation, new reflections on the Catholic doctrine of original sin and are speaking of yet unfinished tasks for the Catholic theology of original sin. In every effort to take the biblical testimony into consideration, dogmatics begins methodically with the proclamations of the extraordinary magisterium and tries to interpret the relevant Bible passages in their light.

However, since nearly all the statements of the magisterium stem from a time which did not have today's insights into Holy Scripture and, in particular, into literary form, it must be admitted that in coordinating dogma and scripture the exegetical findings of the present are too little applied. As an examination of the scripture passages will show, scripture teaches the origin and propagation of sin only so explicitly as to say that after the creation of mankind sin entered the world and spread quickly; the idea of inheriting sin is not a biblical concept. Sin exercises on earth a tyrannical power that only a stronger power can conquer. This stronger power is the salvation of Jesus

Christ. Mankind under the power of sin (amartia: Rom. 5: 12f., 20f.) is mankind outside of Christ; mankind under the power of grace (charis: Rom. 5: 15, 17, 20f.) is mankind in Christ. It can thus be said that the Catholic doctrine of original sin is nothing other than an attempt to describe theologically the situation of mankind outside of Christ.[39]

The method to be followed in a reinterpretation of the Catholic doctrine of original sin seems to demand, not that we try to interpret the Bible in the light of the dogma, but that we interpret the dogma in the light of the Bible. An attempt to use this method follows.

III

The Outbreak of Sin Among Men
According to Genesis 1-11

We take for granted here that revelation in the Bible (although what it says about the salvation that God has prepared for men is, in the final analysis, a unified whole) has been expressed in many different modes of human thought. This is true not only of the New Testament (compare, for example, the way salvation appears in the representations of the synoptic gospels, in Paul, and in John) but also of the Old. Within the framework of this book, the results of Old Testament research, on which there is today hardly any disagreement among competent scholars, may be briefly summed up. For a more thorough study of these questions the reader is referred to the pertinent bibliography.[40] It is common knowledge that in the accounts of

Genesis 1–3 (as in the entire section of stories about the "Beginnings," Gen. 1–11) the Yahwistic and the Priestly traditions both have a share. We owe the story of the Fall in Genesis 2: 4b–3: 24 to the Yahwist, and the story of Creation in Genesis 1: 1–2: 4a to the Priestly Document.[41] Since revelation in the Bible is dependent on different human ways of thought and expression it is at once widened and limited.

When we look at the different presentations of the divine plan of salvation, they together give a picture of impressive and colorful variety. When we set them side by side, however, their human limitation comes to the fore; when they are contrasted, the temporal presentation stands out even more sharply against the background of eternal truth. The role that law plays in justification can be understood only when the Epistle of James is compared with the Pauline teaching; in the New Testament, accounts of the Easter event can be more easily seen when we compare the individual witnesses in the New Testament writings with one another. In the same way, the different human modes of thinking through which the revelation of Genesis 1–3 is expressed prove that while the revelation that men have tried to understand in many ways is in itself limitless, *what has been revealed* is strictly limited. Exegesis can certainly say a good deal about the account in Genesis 1: 1–2: 4a which shows the creation of the world and of men as a six-day work. Exegesis can speak about the linguistic form of the text, about its historical, cultural and religio-historical background, its composition, its literary form and the intention and interests of its author. But the fundamental revealed truth that the account expresses can be summed up in one sentence: the whole universe was created by God. Whoever believes this responds to the whole and entire revelation that the story presents. The passage demands no more.

THE PRIESTLY DOCUMENT (P)

Here we find ourselves at the heart of the problem: what does the priestly account of creation intend to say? What doctrine does it teach? It is generally recognized today that this document leaves the question about *how* God created man completely open; it limits itself to saying that God *did* create man. The story speaks of the creation of plants and animals as the creation of kinds of beings (not of individuals), and it speaks of the creation of humans in the same way. *Naaseh adam* (1:26) means "let us make mankind"; *wayyibra elohim et-ha-adam* (1: 27) means "and God made mankind."[42] For this reason, those who would like to relate the monogenism-polygenism problem to the Bible must give up any attempt to use the Priestly Document as a proof text.[43] If it could be cited at all, the Priestly Document probably speaks more for polygenism.

But even this would be to misuse the text because the Bible never thought about this problem.[44] It is an established exegetical fact that when the Priestly Document speaks of man as created in the image of God it does not mean that man was furnished with supernatural powers; it refers, rather, to the essence of man as a morally responsible personality.[45] That man was created in the image of God is specifically reaffirmed after the flood (Gen. 9: 6). Man did not lose this through sin.

A more difficult question to answer is: how does P see the *quality* of creation? He repeatedly emphasizes in his account of creation that everything that God made was good (1: 3, 10, 12, 18, 21, 25) and at the end he has God give his final judgment that creation was very good (1: 31). In the entire genealogy between Adam and Noah we find no indications of sin.[46]

Then we are surprised by the summary statement that the earth was corrupt in God's sight and that it was filled with violence because all flesh had corrupted their way upon the earth (6: 11f.). Sin seems to have sprung up suddenly like tares in the field, and to have spread with remarkable speed. We are not told how sin entered mankind. P doesn't mention it. Concerning the origin of *sin,* P exercises the same reserve as when speaking of the origin of *man.* As, in the final analysis, it is only said that man comes from God, so also in the final analysis it is only said that sin doesn't come from God, who created the world good, but from man: "all *flesh* had corrupted their way upon the earth" (6: 12), "the earth is filled with violence *through them*" (because of men, or by men) (6: 13). With all possible certainty sin and its consequences are here attributed to man. Sin is here emphatically described as *hamas* (v. 11, 13). *Hamas* is autocratic and unjust behaviour to a fellow man. Sarah complains to Abraham of Hagar's *hamas* after Hagar has conceived a child and, therefore, triumphs over Sarah (16: 5). Often, however, *hamas* means a bloody deed, and P knows well that even this is not lacking among the sins of mankind (9: 5).

It is clear that the priestly theology is particularly preoccupied with the problem of sin. This problem is intensified as God comes down closer and closer to mankind, first in the covenant with Noah, then with Abraham. Finally, with Moses, he pitches his tent among his people in order to be henceforth an ever-present revelation in their midst. The presence of the holy God in the midst of sinful mankind creates a cleavage which Moses bridges by establishing the sacrificial cult at Yahweh's command—a central point in the P story. Surely, the priestly theology cannot have ignored the question of how sin came into the world after God had made the world so good. Did God from the beginning make the human heart incline to evil so as to resist God and put its own will in the place of God's will? P doesn't say, and this doesn't surprise us when we think how painfully P tries to maintain a distance between the holy God and a sinful mankind. Here, as elsewhere, the impulsive Yahwist has simplified when he has God excuse sin with the statement: "the imagination of man's heart is evil from his youth" (8: 21). In the language of today's theology we might say that God made man good at heart, but also weak.

THE STORY OF PARADISE AND
THE FALL (J)

The author of the Yahwistic account in Genesis 2: 4b-3: 24 moves in a world of totally different language and images. In contrast to the teaching of P, he wants to be understood by the common people. But this has been so often and so convincingly demonstrated that we need not go into it here.[47] Nevertheless, we must not overlook the fact that the theology of the Yahwist is, in the final analysis, that of P as well as that of the prophets. We find this theology in its first spontaneity in the Yahwistic document and in its maturest form in P.[48] Certainly the priestly circle in Jerusalem, whose theology in the P document took shape about 500 B.C., knew the Yahwistic work—a work likewise originating in Judah but about half a millenium older.[49] But P does not simply take over J; rather, P permits itself slight deviations. When P does deviate, however, he does not do so arbitrarily; instead he makes an attempt to clarify an older tradition in the light of an advancing revelation.

The priestly account, then, contains an attempt to give within the Bible itself an exegesis of an older tradition, namely, that of the Yahwistic paradise story. Thus P can help us to sift the binding doctrinal content from its form which does not bind.[50] Therefore, we may count on finding in J the same teaching as we found in P. This is true, first of all, of the account of the creation of mankind. Without any doubt, the description in Genesis 2: 27 of God forming man from the dust of the earth and breathing the breath of life into his nostrils is a picturesque presentation. It does not try to say anything binding about the way man came into existence. It speaks, rather, about his ultimate origin and his essence. He was created by God and received his life from God's life. Nevertheless, he is of mortal stuff and must one day return to earth. This necessity is already hinted at in his creation before sin enters the picture. After the Fall it will be mentioned again (3: 19). Needless to say, the Yahwistic story of the creation of man cannot be cited either for or against the theory of evolution.

At first glance, "man" *(ha adam),* whose creation is told of in 2: 7, seems to mean, clearly, a masculine individual, for the creation of the feminine individual is recounted later on (2: 18–24). From this first human couple all mankind is descended. But J has, in his turn, used different sources in the composition of his work. He had to collect the materials that he incorporated into his story from many Israelite traditions, and the task of tying these stories together into a single work was not accomplished without difficulties and discrepancies.

Although the Yahwist was a master storyteller, he could not master his varied materials completely. Actually, we do find such lack of harmony in the story of the Fall, which makes its exegesis very difficult.[51] In fact, we can hardly avoid the conclusion that the story of the creation of the woman was originally an independent story. We cannot help noticing that the divine prohibition comes before the creation of the woman (2:16) but that the snake later asks the *woman* exactly how the prohibition was worded (3:1). Clearly, the woman must have been present in 2:16ff. Verse 3:24 says that "the man" *(ha adam),* in the singular, was driven from the garden although undoubtedly both the man *and* the woman were driven out. "Man's" being driven out of the garden corresponds to "man's" being set into the garden in Genesis 2:8, and we can conclude from this that originally "man" included man and woman.

Finally, we notice that in the story about the creation of the woman the man gives his wife the name "woman" *(issah).* The author takes for granted then that the man himself is named "man" (is) and not "mankind" (adam) as the present text has it.

These observations justify the conclusion that the Yahwist found the story of the creation of the woman (2:18–24) as a separate tradition. At the same time, in the other source from which he took the sentence: "then the Lord God formed man of dust from the ground, and breathed into his nostrils the breath of life; and man became a living being" (Gen. 2:7), *ha adam* means not a single masculine individual but mankind as a species and in both sexes. (In fact, Adam always has a collective sense in Hebrew.)[52] But in the temptation story (3:1–7) a woman plays the leading role.[53] Thus the Yahwist thought himself permitted to place the narration of the creation of the woman (2: 18–24), a story then well-know in Israel, before the temptation story. After that, *ha adam* in 2:7 could be understood only as a masculine individual. The text seems to have developed thus: the Israelite tradition knew of the creation of mankind.

Side by side with this story there existed a popular tale about the creation of the woman from one of the man's ribs, an aetiology (a story explaining causes) to explain why man and wife in marriage could become one flesh— because they originally were one flesh.[54] When this story was incorporated by the Yahwist in his work the old tradition about the creation of mankind became individualized. We have already seen how important it was to the priestly theology to compensate for this and limit itself to the statement that mankind was created by God. It is thus inadmissible to see Genesis 2: 7 as a biblical teaching of monogenism. As often as different authors speak and different currents mingle in the Pentateuch and in the Old and New Testaments, so often stands one voice against another voice and one view against another view. But the ten-

sion is never resolved, and the contradictions are never unified. Such findings show us that the revealing spirit did not
want to make any univocal and binding statement on the
subject, and we are thus forbidden to draw stringent conclusions by hearing one side and neglecting the other.

DONA PRAETURNATURALIA?

What about the so-called preternatural gifts of man before
the Fall? These have led a notoriously tenacious existence
in Catholic theology as the earlier quotations from cate-
chetic and dogmatic works show (in particular the new
German *Einheitskatechismus,* p. 30). But a careful exegesis
shows that here also too much has been demanded of the
biblical text.

It has always been hard to understand why the first man
succumbed so quickly to temptation and believed so blindly
in what the tempter dangled before his eyes, in spite of the
fact that his understanding had been especially enlightened,
his will furnished with special strength, his desires and
aspirations directed wholly towards the good, and he himself free from inclination to evil. The moment the snake
called the woman's attention to the forbidden tree, desire
immediately awoke within her, and the act was committed
without delay. There is not the slightest trace in the story
of qualms of conscience, of an inner conflict or of hesitation

to sin. Sin became practically inevitable for the first man when he played with temptation.

The opinion has become more and more accepted by theologians that the Fall did not alter man's physical characteristics but rather, his relations with God and with his fellow man.[55] It would be a mistake in method for the theologian to give up the traditional teachings about the preternatural gifts only under pressure from the natural sciences, as often seems to happen. Rather, a knowledge of what the J author intends to say ought to be gained by the use of exegetical methods.

When the judgment on the woman runs: "I will greatly multiply your pain in childbearing; in pain you shall bring forth children, yet your desire shall be for your husband, and he shall rule over you," the author cannot have intended to say that the woman must take on numerous pregnancies. Her punishment lies rather in the contradictions of her existence; she cannot leave her husband although she has nothing more to expect from him than tyranny, labor pains and worries about the children. Her sorrow is that in the ancient Near Eastern culture in which the story-teller lived she is good for nothing more than to bear children to her husband.[56] To read into this passage freedom from physical pain for man in his original state— this passage is after all the only slender piece of evidence there is to support the traditional position—is to miss its real meaning entirely. The same holds true of the judgment or curse on the man. His punishment does not mean that work has become hard for him. The significant point is contained in the words: "Cursed is the ground because of you; in toil you shall eat of it all the days of your life; thorns and thistles it shall bring forth to you; and you shall eat the plants of the field."

A cleavage runs through the existence of the man as well as through that of the woman. As the woman is at the mercy of the man, although he makes her life one of trouble and sorrow, so is the man dependent for subsistence on the earth, although the earth's thorns and thistles fill his life with trouble and sorrow. He cannot escape this fate. It pursues him to the end of his life until he returns to the earth from which he was taken.

Therefore the doctrine of the original freedom from suffering for man has no exegetical basis.[57] The so-called curses (3: 14–19) reflect rather the human situation, a situation grounded in the nature of man and independent of whether he sins or not. The Yahwist brings these circumstances into relation with sin because he wants to show that it is *sin* which drives man into sorrow and helplessness, causing the cleavage in his life which turns human existence into tragedy. In this way the Yahwistic theology gives hints of the hope of redemption which is central in the Old Testament and in his work in particular. Through sin man has reached a situation in which he can no longer help himself. Help can come to him only through the saving act of God.

DEATH—PUNISHMENT FOR SIN?

There are even today open-minded exegetes who believe that an exception must be made to the above fundamental understanding of the curses. Death *must* be a consequence of sin.[58] A two-fold exegetical finding, however, speaks against this idea. In the first place, all the "curses" are constructed on the same unified principle, and it is hard to see why they should not all be understood on the same unified principle.[59] If the other "curses"—the snake's crawling upon his belly, the woman's labor pains and dependence on her husband, the man's labor for his daily bread—are in reality no punishment but man's natural situation, then the same must be true of death. In this case the verse concerning death does not form part of the curse. The curse of the man means that the earth is accursed; that it brings forth thorns and thistles; that man eats his bread in the sweat of his brow *until* he returns to earth. Only death will put an end to the cares of his life. "Until" limits this time. The end, his return to earth, has simply been taken for granted. It was, as we have seen, already hinted at when man was created (2: 7) and is reinforced here.[60] If we wanted to consider death as a curse, then, thinking logically, it would have to apply only to the man and not to the woman.

Two further verses are often cited in support of death as a punishment, 2: 17 and 3: 22. In 2: 17 God adds to the prohibition of eating of the tree of knowledge the threat "for the day you eat of it, you shall (or must) surely die"— so the verse is usually translated. But a careful philological investigation gives us a much more complete understanding of the verse. The Hebrew *beyom* (literally "on the day") can also have the general meaning "when" or "if." In addition, the formal phrase "you shall surely die" means that this deed is punishable by death. It does not follow that this person would otherwise never have died or that he absolutely must be so punished after the act.[61]

In 3: 22 the author has God speak his final judgment on mankind: "And he said, 'Indeed, the man has become like one of us, knowing good and evil. And perhaps he will put forth his hand and take also of the tree of life, and eat and live forever . . .'" Then God banishes man from the vicinity of the tree of life to keep him from eating of it and thereby living eternally. Before the Fall, it is argued, man would have been allowed to eat of the tree of life. He would have lived forever. However, the clearly mythological character of this element in the story prohibits its being used for dogmatic purposes. "This image and this idea stem from the established and widespread longing of man who experiences death as his greatest evil and wants to be immortal like the gods."[62] The Mesopotamian tree-of-life motif plays a completely secondary role in the story of the Fall, and it is difficult to put it on the same level as the principal Palestinian themes of the story.[63]

Therefore, many well-known theologians today are rejecting the concept of the so-called gift of immortality. These scholars certainly do not think they are in conflict with either Romans 5: 12 or with the Synod of Carthage.[64] They do not consider that they conflict with the canon of the Council of Trent which says that Adam, through his sin, drew upon himself the wrath and displeasure of God and thus the death with which God had previously threatened him (D788–DS1511). They also make it clear that the decrees of the Council of Trent on original sin must be understood in the light of the exegetical knowledge that we have today.

In all the rest of the Old Testament we find no indications that death is a consequence of or a punishment for sin, unless, perhaps, in accordance with the Israelite doctrine of retribution a premature death is seen as a punishment for a sinful life. We must be very careful here, as in every discussion of a scriptural passage, not to wrench an individual expression from its context and consider it in isolation. Bearing this warning in mind, we see that the apparently irrefutable verse: "In woman was sin's beginning, and because of her we all die" (Ecclus. 25: 23) has upon closer inspection a much more general sense. "Taken in context this verse shows that Ben Sirach is speaking, as he often does, very personally, and that here he is speaking of immoral women. This is his theme. He is not giving a doctrinal discussion of the consequences of original sin."[65] Ecclesiasticus considers sin as simply part of the human condition. Ben Sirach (17: 1), clearly playing on the verses

Genesis 2:7 and 3:19, says: "The Lord created man of the earth, and turned him into it again. He gave them few days and a short time, and power also over the things therein."[66]

There is another verse often cited on this topic, "But by the envy of the devil death entered the world: and they who are in his possession experience it" (Wis. 2:24). This verse cannot be understood to mean physical death; it can only mean death in the eschatological sense. All men, after all, experience physical death, not just those who belong to the devil. The idea that the sin of Adam is the cause of death appears for the first time in Jewish apocryphal literature (in the fourth book of Esdras, in the Syriac Baruch, in the Vita Adae, and in the Apocalypse of Moses) although contradicted by other sources.[67] The majority of rabbis seem to have held this opinion, but it was contested by others.[68]

THE YAHWIST'S INTEREST IN BEGINNINGS

The succession of pictures with which the Yahwist illustrates the growth of sin upon the earth always impresses the reader of Genesis. After Cain murders his brother, once sin has entered the world, men are no longer afraid to commit even the worst sins (and the slaying of a brother was held by the ancient Semites to be the worse possible sin) until the judgment of God "that the wickedness of man on the earth was great, and that man's every thought and all the imagination of his heart were only evil" (6:5).

The Yahwist and the priestly writer are one in presenting the spread of sin among mankind as rapid, impetuous and unrestrained. The Yahwist has, as we have already seen, this excuse for the lamentable failure of mankind: "for the imagination of man's heart is evil from his youth" (8: 21).[69] The Yahwist is, however, different from the Priestly Document in that he gives us a *story* of the first sin, whereas P tells us only in general terms about the beginning and spread of sin. We know already what a lively interest the Yahwist has in the "beginnings" of whatever is characteristic of the human situation. Cain, for example, is the first farmer (4: 2) after Yahweh has driven man out of the garden to work in the fields (3: 23). After Cain has been driven from the fields, he founds the first city (4: 17). Jabal is the first shepherd (4: 20), Jubal, the first musician (4: 21), Tubal Cain is the first smith (4: 22). At the time when Enoch is born the worship of Yahweh begins (4: 26). Noah is the first to raise grapes and make wine (9: 20); Nimrod is the first tyrant in the world (10: 8). So we should not be surprised that the Yahwist was familiar with a tradition which told how and through whom the first sin was committed, and that he with his subtle knowledge of the human heart and his astounding power of representation made this story into one of the most stirring in the Bible.

We are also not surprised that the theology of the Priestly Document believed itself able to do without this display and to limit itself to the sober remark that sin began among men and grew quickly. If certain theologians are urgent in maintaining the historicity of the Fall in Genesis 3 because they believe that the historicity of salvation through Jesus Christ stands or falls with it, then we ought to make a clear distinction here. We must distinguish between the historicity of the beginning of sin among mankind with its rapid spread to all humanity on the one hand, and the historicity of the details of the paradise story, including the representation of Adam and Eve as the parents of the whole human race, on the other.[70] The biblical and ecclesiastical teaching on redemption seems to demand the historicity of the former but not the historicity of the latter.[71]

For the Bible the appearance of sin is less a temporal than an ontological and theological event. Although the Holy Scriptures say clearly that sin came into the world through human fault, they are not so clear as to when and how this happened. The biblical writers did not have, after all, any private revelation about prehistoric times, and they could not lean on a revelation handed down from the beginning.[72] Rather, they drew on popular traditions of Israel and of neighboring peoples in the ancient Near East and interpreted and presented these traditions in the light of the religious history of Israel. "Revelation must here mean, more or less," says Renckens,[73] "that Israel reconstructed the first happenings on one hand through a supernaturally enlightened reflection on the powerful historical experiences that Israel had had with Yahweh, and on the other hand through a practical and speculative battle, lasting hundreds of years, with the great problems of life and in particular with the problem of evil." As has been frequently noticed, the story of the Fall in Genesis 3 finds no echo in the entire Old Testament.

Certainly the universality of sin is one of the basic theses of prophetic theology, "For there is no man who does not sin" (I Kings 8:46). The prophets see the people ensnared by sin; sin has become second nature to them. "Can the Ethiopian change his skin, or the leopard his spots? Then also you can do good who are accustomed to do evil," says Jeremiah (13:23). But this deep and universal sinfulness is never related to Adam,[74] and the thought that sin is transmitted by physical generation is quite foreign to the Old Testament.[75] Certainly the Old Testament understands solidarity in curse and blessing, understands the influence of the individual for good or evil.[76] This individual can be a "father," in the broadest sense of the word, but he *need* not be. Furthermore, we must not forget that in the language of the Old Testament the concepts "seed," "beget," "bear," "and "son" often have not a physical but a moral, geographical, or national sense.[77] If this were not so the correspondence between Adam and Christ developed by Paul in Romans 5:12–21 would have no meaning. If the apostle had based his comparison on the biological relation of mankind to Adam, then he would have had to say that salvation in Jesus Christ necessitates a biological relation to

Christ. But no one has ever had that idea. Consequently, when Karl Rahner says that the scriptures seem throughout to take for granted that the community of men for good or evil has a biological basis, a look at what the Bible actually says convinces us of the exact opposite.

IV

The Adam-
Christ Parallel in Paul

ROMANS 5:12-21:

The position of mankind mired in sin was hopeless; salvation could come only through a saving act of God.[78] That this saving act happened in Christ and completely changed the situation of mankind is the argument of the apostle Paul in Romans 5: 12–21, the *locus classicus* of the doctrine of original sin. The basic statement which will be discussed in this chapter begins with verse 12:

Dia touto hosper di enos anthropou he hamartia eis ton cosmon eiselthen, kai dia tes hamartias ho thanatas, kai houtos eis pantas anthropous ho thanatas dielthen, eph ho pantes hemarton.

Therefore as through one man sin entered into the world
and through sin death, and thus death has passed unto all
men because all have sinned.

Sicut per unum hominem peccatum in hunc mundum
intravit, et per peccatum mors, et ita omnes homines
mors transiit, in quo omnes peccaverunt. (Vulgate)

We must first maintain that in this verse, as in the entire
section, no idea of a biological unity with Adam can be
found.[79] Rather, a moral causality and responsibility for all
mankind is attributed to Adam as the originator of sin.
"Paul begins"—we should not expect him to do otherwise
—"with the story of the Fall as told in Genesis 2 and 3,
and interprets the story in the manner of the contemporary
Jewish theology."[80] Certainly, a literal understanding of this
story does not belong to the object of the Pauline teaching
any more than the literal understanding of the story of
Jonah is the object of Jesus' teaching. When Jesus says that
the Son of Man will be three days and nights in the heart
of the earth as Jonah was three days and nights in the belly
of the whale (Matt. 12: 40),[81] he does not intend his words
to be taken literally. Although Paul leans heavily on the
contemporary Jewish exegesis of Genesis 2ff., he does depart
from it in one decisive point. While in Jewish exegesis
(compare in particular Wisdom 2: 24, the passage Paul
undoubtedly has in mind) the death of all was a conclusion
drawn from the sin of Adam (in accord with the usual

understanding of Genesis 2ff.), Paul attributes to Adam's sin the effect *that sin came into the world* and *from sin came the death that everyone suffers.*[82] When the sin as personified by Paul succeeded in penetrating into the world its victory was already assured. At the moment of its entrance it had already taken up rule over mankind. The moment of its entrance into the world was the moment it seized power and was enthroned.[83] Thus, Paul is in perfect agreement as to content with the Yahwistic and priestly theology.

The concept of sin or death as *inherited* is not mentioned at all by Paul.[84] Of sin he says that it came into the world (eiselthen) and reached (dielthen) all men. Sin came into the world (Heb. 10:5, eiserchomenos; John 1:9, erchomenon eis ton cosmon). Its power of expansion reached all men, and so death came to all men.[85] Physical death cannot be the primary meaning of the universal death which is the consequence of sin.[86] Paul uses it in its meaning, for contemporary Jewish views, as a sign of loss of a life of communion with God. In verse 21 *eternal* life (zoe aionios) is explicitly opposed to death (thanatos). "Death" might be taken in the whole section as a paraphrase of "sin." Thus Paul can say at one time that the sin of Adam had as its consequence the sinfulness (hamartia) of all (v. 12); at another time the death of all (vv. 15, 17); at another time the judgment (katakrina) of all (v. 18); and the opposite of judgment is "life-giving justification"[87] (diakaiosis zoes: v. 18). If we were to understand death here as physical death the Adam-Christ antithesis would lose its point because Christ *did not* remove physical death from the world. Moreover, we should not overlook the fact that Paul, in Romans 5: 12, refers to Wisdom 2: 24 where as we have seen death means "eschatological death."[88]

The last phrase of verse 12, "eph ho pantes hemarton," has played a decisive role in the traditional teaching on original sin. Its role was determined by the Latin translation "in quo omnes peccaverunt," "in whom all have sinned." "In quo" can only be understood to refer to Adam and this resulted in the doctrine that *in Adam* all men have sinned. From Augustine to humanism, about a thousand years, this reading was uncontested in the Latin church. Today, Erasmus' realization that the Greek "eph ho" has the sense of "because" or "considering that" is generally accepted.[89] Therefore we should translate this phrase: "Through one man sin entered into the world and through sin, death, and thus death has passed to all men *because* all men have sinned."

Through the sin of Adam death and sin began to rule in the world. Their power truly brought men under their rule. And because all men were sinners all became liable to death. Nothing justifies us in understanding "sin" in the phrase "since all have sinned" other than the way we have understood it in the first phrase "sin entered the world," namely, sin as an evil deed wilfully committed. Even in the rushing torrent of sin the personal decision of each man was maintained. In reality, the idea of the passive participation of all Adam's descendants in the sin of Adam is far from Paul's mind, and it is not permissible to read this idea into verse 12 by understanding "because all have sinned" in the sense of "because all (in Adam) have become sinful." The verb hamartano, when used by Paul—or in the entire Bible for that matter—always carries the sense of an action.[90] Verses 13ff. cannot be made to say what most exegetes read into it: Between Adam and Moses there were no formal sins, only material sins which consequently did not count as sins. Nevertheless, men died; that is, they were punished with Adam's punishment for sin because they, although without personal guilt, shared in Adam's sin.[91]

S. Lyonnet has convincingly shown that the apostle was quite unaware of this modern problem.[92] His thought is rather this: all men, after Adam sinned, are subject to death because all have committed sinful deeds (v. 12cd). But we know that between Adam and Moses there was sin in the world (13a). The objection runs: without the law, which had then not yet been given, sin could not be imputed to anyone according to Paul's own teaching (4: 15).[93] We should, then, expect that men in those times did not die; that is, were not subject to the punishment of sin (v. 13b.). But, in reality, death had power over men in the time between Adam and Moses, even if they had not, like Adam, acted against a direct prohibition of God (5: 14a). This proves for Paul that there was no time after Adam at which man did not commit individual, personal sins (hamarte-santas).[94] There seems to be no teaching of original sin here.[95]

The sinful deed of Adam which Paul calls parabasis "transgression" (v. 14) or paraptoma "sin" (vv. 15–18) or parakon "disobedience" (v. 19), stands opposed to the saving act of Jesus Christ which the apostle calls dikaioma, "righteous deed" (v. 18) and hupakon "obedience" (v. 19). These expressions can refer only to Jesus' death on the cross (cf. Phil. 2: 8, "he humbled himself and became obedient unto death, even death on a cross").[96]

Christ's death on the cross is his enthronement over the kingdom of grace which now replaces the kingdom of sin and death. But if the kingdom of sin and death can have no power in each person unless that person decides to accept it, so also the kingdom of grace. Only "those who receive (lambanoutes in the sense of *accept*)[97] the abundance of grace and the free gift of righteousness reign in life through the one man Jesus Christ" (v. 17).[98] Verse 19 should also be understood in this sense: "For as by one man's disobedience many were made sinners,[99] so by one man's obedience many will be made righteous." In fact, grace is nearer to them than sin and death were before (cf. pallo mallon in v. 15). But grace is no more inherited than sin and death were previously inherited.

TRADITION AND MAGISTERIUM

K. H. Schelkle has presented the history of the exegesis of Romans 5:12-21.[100] The first coherent Latin exegesis, that of Ambrosiaster, interprets Romans 5:12 *"in quo, id est in Adam, omnes peccaverunt."*[101] Augustine turns for this exegesis to the "holy Hilary" to whom he apparently gives credit for Ambrosiaster's commentary. It must certainly be said, however, that Augustine read more of his teaching on original sin into the passage than he could have got from it. S. Lyonnet has been able to show that until the beginning of the Pelagian controversy, Augustine, although his teaching on original sin had been fully developed for a long time, quoted the phrase "in quo omnes peccaverunt" only three times in all,[102] and that he cited it without making any connection with original sin.

It is likewise true that Augustine, during the Pelagian controversy, based his doctrine of original sin on Romans 5:12, and he made the mistake of taking the "in quo" of the Latin translation he had before him as a relative. What is worse, Augustine did not find *mors* as the subject of *pertransiit* in his Bible. Consequently, he assumed that *peccatum* was the subject because such an emendation fitted beautifully into the opinion he already had formed. From this ground he fought the Pelagians, who were using the correct Greek text which gave the equivalent of *mors pertransiit.*[103] In ignorance of the complete Greek text and being spontaneously inclined to read "peccatum pertransiit," he took the following "in quo" to refer to the "peccatum" he had supplied, and so the one sin of Adam became the sin of all men.[104] In his writing *Contra Julianum,* he sums up his interpretation of Romans 5: 12 as follows:

> Nam ego per unum hominem in mundum intrasse peccatum, et per peccatum mortem, et ita in omnes homines pertransisse (no subject), in quo peccaverunt omnes, ab initio conversionis meae sic tenui semper et teneo.[105] (I hold, and since the beginning of my conversion have ever held, that through one man sin entered into the world and through sin, death, and thus (no subject) spread to all men, in whom all have sinned.)

His interpretation, together with the whole weight of this personal confession of faith, entered into the history of Latin theology, and it lies at the basis of the Council of Trent's decree on original sin.

An understanding of this Tridentine decree demands, more than any other, a knowledge of what went before it.[106] We see how controversial the problem of original sin was. We see how important the Tridentine fathers thought it when we remember that the council, postponing all other problems, took up this one first in its fifth session after it had mastered the basic topic "Scripture and Tradition" in the fourth session. To be sure of being able to handle the decree on original sin in the fifth session, set for June 17th, 1546, the legates strove to finish the provisional schemas in great haste. To facilitate this, Cardinal del Monte had proposed in the general congregation of the previous May 28th that they collect and go through everything that their predecessors had decreed on this subject, either at ecumenical councils or at provincial councils that had been approved by the church, and that whatever seemed necessary for the present moment then be added, "so that, by renewing the ancient decrees and adding new considerations, this sacred council's decree on this matter may be as helpful as possible."[107]

Among the decisions of earlier councils, the most important were Canon 2 of the Council of Carthage in 418 (D102–DS223) and the first and second canons of the Council of Orange in 529 (D147f.–DS371f.). The influence that these two councils exercised on the Tridentine decree on original sin had a doubly disadvantageous effect: first, the Tridentine decree was in reality directed more against the Pelagians than against the reformers; and second, the Council of Trent renounced any attempt to define original sin, although there existed, even among the Catholic theologians themselves, the greatest diversity and uncertainty.[108] In this way, the council abstained from any positive formulation of the doctrine of original sin and limited itself to the negative form the canon now has.

This explains how the second canon of the Council of

Trent (D789–DS1512) duplicates the second canon of the Council of Orange to a great extent in its form and entirely in its content. After the publication of this decree of the fifth session of Trent many voices asked whether it had been necessary or useful for the council to busy itself with the errors of Pelagius, condemned more than a thousand years before.[109]

In studying the Tridentine decree on original sin we must keep in mind not only that the council could not have known the problems that we in the twentieth century have, but also that it met the problems of the sixteenth century to a large extent with formulations taken from the dogmatic difficulties of the fifth and sixth centuries. This last point especially demands that we handle the Tridentine canon on original sin with extraordinary historical and theological tact. In addition, the biblical-exegetical insights that we have today can lead us to a more exact knowledge than earlier generations had about what in this decree is binding and lasting doctrinal teaching, and what must be recognized as a transitory view serving as a vehicle for the dogma. The council certainly does not want to say more than the Bible says. According to a leading theologian of the present, dogma is "a new formulation of the original revelation in the consciousness of faith *at a particular moment,* a revelation which may also find expression in another formulation, in the consciousness of faith of another time."[110] If this is true, the development of exegesis cannot be without meaning for an understanding of revelation.

The scriptures are witness that once sin entered the

world, it spread among men like a rushing torrent with such power that, in spite of personal freedom, no man in reality could escape it. When a man, furnished only with human powers, was born into the sinful world, he became, at the same time, subject to the might of sin. It is in this sense that Adam transmitted "sin which is the death of the soul to all mankind" ("peccatum, quod mors est animae, in omne genus humanum transfudisse," D789–DS1512).[111] When the following canon (D790–DS1513) states that "Adae peccatum . . . propagatione, non imitatione, transfusum omnibus inest" ("The sin of Adam, transmitted by generation, not by imitation, is in everyone"), this statement is directed, like the conciliar decree, at the error of Pelagius, according to which Adam is the cause of spiritual death only for those who imitate his fault.[112]

The council thus demands from all men belief not merely in a passive but in an *active* influence of original sin on all men. Every creature having a human nature and belonging to the human race is *personally* affected by the sin of Adam in that he is subject to the might of sin and thus becomes himself a sinner. And so the sin of Adam is multiplied in his posterity.[113] Man cannot attain the state of grace, the state of being a child of God (cf. D796–DS1524) through the powers of human nature or any other means, but only through the merits of the one mediator, our Lord, Jesus Christ (D790–DS1513). Through his death he took away not only the sin of Adam, but the sin of the world ("qui *nos* deo reconciliavit in sanguine suo,") "who has reconciled us to God in his blood." (Ibid.)

It is not accidental that the council in the same canon cites John 1:29: "Behold the lamb of God who takes away the sins of the world."[114] In the center of the Tridentine decree on original sin, as in the center of scripture, stands, not the sin of Adam, but the salvation of Jesus Christ.

SUMMARY

The research presented above has the following consequences:

(1) The idea that <u>Adam's descendants</u> are automatically sinners because of the sin of their ancestor, and <u>that they are already sinners when they enter the world, is foreign to Holy Scripture.</u> The well known verse from the psalms, "Behold I was born in iniquity, and in sin did my mother conceive me" (Ps. 51:7, 50:7), merely means that everyone born of woman becomes a sinner in this world, without fail. The Bible often uses the device of attributing a man's later deeds or achievements to him from the time of his conception and birth. (Cf. for example Jeremiah 1:5, where Jeremiah is made a prophet in his mother's womb.)

(2) The "inheritance" of Adam's sin means rather that sin, after its entrance into the world, so spread that consequently all men are born into a sinful world and in this sinful world become themselves sinners.

(3) When the Holy Scriptures speak of the sin of "Adam," this is the expression folklore uses to describe the

entrance of sin into the world. Scripture in no way teaches the descent of the human race from a single human couple when it uses such an expression. Whether mankind originated in monogenism or polygenism is a question which only science can answer; it is not a theological question. The thesis of polygenism cannot be rejected on the basis of original sin.

(4) No man enters the world a sinner. As the creature and image of God he is from his first hour surrounded by God's fatherly love. Consequently, he is not at birth, as is often maintained, an enemy of God and a child of God's wrath. A man becomes a sinner only through his own individual and responsible action.

(5) However, the man who is born in the New Covenant time does not automatically share in the life of the risen Christ. All men are called to this life, but they receive it only when they become united to Christ, become one with him as the branches with the vine (Cf. John 15: 2–7).

(6) This union with the risen Christ is based on faith and becomes effective through baptism. Holy Scripture calls baptism a second birth (Cf. John 3: 3–7). After birth according to the flesh man needs for salvation birth according to the Spirit of God (Cf. John 1: 13 and 3:6).

(7) Thus baptism does not bring about the removal of "original sin," but rather rebirth as a child of God; it makes man a member of Christ. Through it he participates in Christ's life; he is taken up into the community of salvation, into the People of God, into the church. But participation in the life of Christ cannot be reconciled with

sin. Consequently, baptism also becomes, for those who personally have committed sins, a sacrament which takes away sins.

(8) The baptismal rite now used for infants has been taken over from the adult baptismal rite. It thus contains ceremonies of cleansing and exorcism meaningful for the adult, but scarcely for the baby. A new rite for infant baptism should omit them.

(9) The only human being who did not need rebirth or the remission of sins was Mary the mother of Jesus. By anticipation, she lived her entire life in the glory of Christ's grace. This is what we mean when we speak of the "Immaculate Conception," although, admittedly, the expression is not well chosen.

(10) Likewise, the grace of Christ does not spare us the sorrowful experience of living in a sinful world and of falling, ourselves, under the power of sin. The whole sacramental structure of the church is ordered to the needs of sinful people; in other words, Christ takes into consideration the fact that all men are sinners, and the church he founded will remain in its earthly pilgrimage a church of sinners. For our salvation is God's deed; "The weak things of the world has God chosen to put to shame the strong . . . lest any flesh should pride itself before him. *From him* you are in Christ Jesus . . . for sanctification and redemption, so that, just as it is written, 'let him who takes pride, take pride in the Lord'" (I Cor. 1:27–31).

Notes

1 Karl Rahner deals further with this topic in his essay "Theological Reflections on Monogenism" in *Theological Investigations*, I, trans. by Cornelius Ernst (Baltimore, 1961), pp. 224–296.

2 Gen. 2: 5 ought to read Gen. 2: 7.

3 For a comprehensive review see the article "Péché originel" by A. Gaudet and M. Jugie in *DThC,* XII, pp. 275–624. Cf. also J. Gross, *Entstehungsgeschichte des Erbsündendogmas* (Munich, Basel, 1960–1963), 2 vols.

4 6th edition (Munich, 1962).

5 *Münchener Universitätsreden,* new series, Vol. 38 (Munich, 1965).

6 It should be pointed out that with Schmaus "theologian" is always to be understood as "dogmatic theologian"; and that "theology" means for him "dogmatics."

7 "The first man was promised bodily immortality. This is expressly defined as an article of faith by the Council of Trent."

8 *Handbuch Theologischer Grundbegriffe,* I, ed. by H. Fries (Munich, 1962), pp. 293–303.

9 *MüThz,* 15 (1964), pp. 17–57.

10 *Wort und Wahrheit,* 20 (1965), pp. 761–776.

11 Emphasis within these and the following quotations are as in the original.

[12] J. Feiner, J. Trütsch, and F. Böckle, *Theology Today* (Milwaukee, Bruce, 1965).

[13] In this question a theologian ought to confine himself to theological arguments. Moreover, the use of the "metaphysical principle of economy" seems especially questionable here. The impartial observer is immediately impressed by nature's unparalleled wastefulness in reproduction (think, for example that in a single act of human reproduction approximately 350 million male sperm cells are emitted of which at most one is effective). In a survey which a Catholic scientist distributed to a number of the fathers of the Second Vatican Council on the question of monogenism-polygenism, it was confirmed that on biological grounds the tracing back of a species to an original pair led to the gravest difficulties. On the basis of our present scientific knowledge, it is believed that such a species would normally have died out. As can be seen from the observations of nature, monogenism would demand that God work a miracle to keep the human race in existence. This is just what is excluded by the advocates of the principle of economy, cf. K. Rahner, *Theological Investigations,* I, p. 296. Moreover, theologians would also have to take into consideration here the analogy between the natural and the supernatural. An "overflowing richness of grace" (Ephes. 2: 17 and elsewhere) rules in the realm of the supernatural, and according to Thomas Aquinas a single drop of Jesus' blood would have sufficed to save the whole world.

[14] Although recently even exegetes have appealed to the anathema of the Council of Carthage in 418 (D101-DS202) in support of the original immortality of man. Cf. V. Hamp, "Paradies und Tod," *Festschrift J. Schmid* (Regensburg, 1963), pp. 100–109; here 107f.; also R. Koch, *Erlösungstheologie: Genesis 1–11 (Bergen-Enkheim,* 1965), p. 75. It is satisfying to note that, on the other hand, many theologians today do not share such thoughts. For Pope Zosimus' ostensible approbation of this first canon of Carthage, see the preamble in *DS,* p. 82.

[15] For ages 10–17. The following is taken from *The Confraternity Edition No. 3,* ed. by Francis J. Connell (Paterson, New Jersey, St. Anthony Guild, 1962), pp. 33–37; Cf. also the *New Revised Edition No. 2,* ed. by Michael A. McGuire. (New York, Benzinger Brothers, 1962).

[16] *College Texts in Theology,* Vol. I, *God and His Creation,* ed. by William B. Murphy, O.P., *et al.,* (Dubuque, Priory Press, 1958), p. 390.

[17] p. 398f. The following methodological remark should be noted (p. 398 n. 12): "On the whole, if one wishes to dispute the scholastic claims for Adam, it will have to be on other grounds than the lack of historical proof."

[18] p. 400f.

[19] p. 402f.

[20] pp. 403–405.

[21] p. 406.

[22] *The Living Faith* (New York, Herder & Herder, 1966), pp. 38–42. *A Catholic Catechism* (New York, Herder & Herder, 1957), pp. 38–42.

[23] Romans 5: 12, as given in the original German edition of the catechism, reads: *"weil alle* (in Adam) *gesündigt haben"* (p. 37), "because all have sinned (in Adam)." *The Living Faith* uses the words of the Confraternity translation of the New Testament, leaving out "in Adam" with the explanation "All men have got to die because Adam, who was the first man, committed sin." *The Living Faith,* p. 323. *A Catholic Catechism,* III, 83.

[24] *The Living Faith,* p. 42f. *A Catholic Catechism,* I, p. 42f.

[25] Brother J. Frederick and Brother H. Albert (Chicago, Regnery, 1965), I, p. 26.

[26] *On Our Way Series, Vatican II Edition,* by Sr. Maria de la Cruz, Rev. Francis J. Buckley, S.J., Sr. Laetitia Bordes, Rev. Cyr Miller.

[27] I, pp. 18–30.

[28] II, pp. 18–23.

[29] III, p. 3.

[30] V, p. 6.

[31] VI, pp. 9–13.

[32] VII, p. 36.

[33] VIII, pp. 39, 133.

[34] The above citations are from the first *On Our Way Series* (New York, Sadlier, 1958–1964), 8 vols.

[35] *Bible Life and Worship Series* (Boston, Allyn & Bacon, 1965).

[36] *A New Catechism* (New York, Herder & Herder, 1967).

[37] e.g. A. Vanneste, *NRTh,* 87 (1965), pp. 715–7117.

[38] According to A. Vanneste (*ibid.,* p. 715), numerous theories have been invented ("inventées") to explain this.

[39] *Ibid.,* p. 717.

[40] Introductions to the Old Testament: A. Lods (Paris, 1950); H. H. Rowley (Oxford, 1951); (London[2], 1952); A. Robert and A. Tricot (New York, 1960); Robert Pfeiffer (New York, 1948); P. J. Cools (Utrecht, Antwerp 1957), German edition (Olten, 1965); Aage Bentzen (Copenhagen[5], 1959); A. Robert and A. Feuillet (Tournai[2], 1959); C. Kuhl (Bern[2], 1960); A. Weiser (New York, 1961); E. Sellin and G. Fohrer (Heidelberg[10], 1965).

Selected Literature on Genesis: B. Vawter, *A Path through Genesis* (New York, 1956) and (London, 1957); B. Gemser *et alii, Studies on the Book of Genesis, Oudtestamentische Studien,* 12 (Leiden, 1958); O. Eissfeldt, *Die Genesis der Genesis* (Tübingen[2], 1961); M. Noth, *Überlieferungsgeschichte des Pentateuch* (Stuttgart[2], 1963); J.-P. Bouhot and H. Cazelles, "Pentateuque," *DBS,* VII, pp. 687–858.

Commentaries on the Book of Genesis: J. Chaine (Paris, 1948); E. König (Gütersloh, 1925); A. Clamer (Paris, 1953); H. Junker (Würzburg[4], 1958); G. von Rad (London[3], 1961); R. de Vaux (Paris[2], 1962); J. de Fraine (Roermond, 1963); H. Gunkel (Göttingen⁶, 1964); H. Cassuto, English trans. (Jerusalem, Vol. I, Vol. II, 1964).

To Gen. 1–11: P. Humbert *Études sur le récit du Paradis et de la chute dans la Genèse* (Neuchâtel, 1940); C. Hauret, *Origines, Genèse 1–3* (Paris 1950) and "Origines" in *DBS*, VI, pp. 908–926; G. Lambert, "Le Drame du Jardin d'Eden" *NRth*, 76 (1954), pp. 917–948, 1044–1072; W. Zimmerli, I Mose, 1–11 (Zürich², 1957); H. Renckens, *Israëls visie op het verleden* (Tielt and The Hague, 1957), Eng. trans., *Israel's Concept of the Beginning* (New York, 1964); F. Hvidberg, "The Canaanite Background of Genesis 1–3," *VT*, 10 (1960), pp. 285–294; T. Schwegler, *Die biblische Urgeschichte im Lichte der Forschung* (Munich², 1962); W. H. Schmidt, *Die Schöpfungsgeschichte der Priesterschrift* (Neukirchen and Vluyn, 1964).

[41] One story is called Yahwistic because it uses the name Yahweh for God from the beginning of time onwards, although according to the Israelite tradition this name was first revealed to Moses (Ex. 3: 13–15 and 6: 2f.). The other is called the Priestly Tradition since it is easy to see that it originated in the priestly circles of the Jerusalem temple. The third tradition of stroies which is found in the first four books of the Pentateuch (Gen.-Num.), the so-called Elohistic Tradition (E), begins only in Genesis 15. It docs not seem to know any story of creation, and therefore is also ignorant of the Fall.

[42] Cf. W. H. Schmidt, *op. cit.,* pp. 144f, 181f. The same interpretation is presented from the Catholic side by, among others, C. Hauret, *op. cit.,* pp. 83–85; A. Clamer, *op. cit.,* p. 112; H. Renckens, *Israel's Concept of the Beginning,* p. 105f.; J. de Fraine, *La Bible et l'origine de l'homme* (Bruges, 1961), pp. 34–40; R. de Vaux, *op. cit.,* p. 42; J. B. Bauer, *Die biblische Urgeschichte* (Paderborn², 1964) p. 32f.

[43] Even K. Rahner, "Theological Reflections on Monogenism,"

op. cit., p. 252, although in the above-mentioned article he speaks indiscriminately at times of Gen. 1–3 and Gen. 2–3.

[44] It is noteworthy that where the priestly redactor himself is writing, *adam* is always used collectively (Gen. 1: 26f., 5: 1b, 2: notice the plural construction "created he them" in 1: 27 and 5: 2). In the genealogy 5: 1a, 3ff., however, which P has taken from the Toledoth, "Adam" is understood as the proper name of the first man. G. von Rad makes this pertinent remark: "It seems, therefore, that the priestly school rejected the mythological representation of a particular individual with the name of Adam and tried to formulate in a purely theological way the idea that mankind, we might say 'the' man, was created by God" *Die Priesterschrift im Hexateuch* Stuttgart, 1934), p. 170.

[45] Cf. H. Renckens, *op. cit.*, pp. 104–110: "To be in the image of God is therefore not merely a personal privilege of the first man, but is something which belongs to the human race as such. By the very fact that one is human, one is made in the image of God." (P. 108.) Also see H. Gross, *LthK,* IV, col. 1087f. "Consequently, being made in the image of God does not contain for Genesis the state of justification, but rather an abiding essential relationship of man to God" (col. 1087). Cf. by the same author "Die Gottebenbildlichkeit des Menschen im alten Testament," *Lex tua Veritas,* Festschrift H. Juncker (Trier, 1961), pp 89–100. Similarly, R. de Vaux *op. cit.*, p. 42; and J. Bauer, *op. cit.*, p. 28f., to mention only the Catholic writers on the subject.

[46] People are fond of saying that P wants to express the entrance of sin into the world and increasing human sinfulness through the shortening of the life spans of men (e.g., G. von Rad, *Die Priesterschrift im Hexateuch* (Stuttgart, 1934), p. 171, "The attentive reader notices that in the gradual diminution of the long life spans a certain deterioration had set in." But does the Sethite list (Gen. 5)

really show a decrease in life spans? On the contrary, in the later generations the ages surpass even that of Adam. Adam was 930 years old when he died, Seth 912, Enosh 905, Kenan 910, Mahalalel 895, Jared 962, Methuselah 969 and Lamech 777. Enoch was taken away (v. 23) at the age of 365. A noteworthy but nevertheless still relatively moderate, decrease can be seen in the last name in the list, Lamech.

[47] For literature on the Yahwistic tradition see note 39. In addition, see particularly: A. Robert, *DBS,* IV, pp. 9–12; M. L. Henry, *Jahwist und Priesterschrift* (Stuttgart, 1960); H. W. Wolff, "Das Kerygma des Jahwisten," *EvTh,* 24 (1964), 73–98—*Gesammelte Studien zum alten Testament* (Munich, 1964), pp. 345–373.

[48] See H. Haag in *Mysterium Salutis I,* ed. by J. Feiner and M. Löhrer (Einsiedeln, 1965), pp. 321–323.

[49] The Yahwistic work probably originated in the tenth century B.C.

[50] H. Renckens' remark (*op. cit.,* p. 231) is to the point: "Genesis reduces the anthropomorphic tableaux of Genesis 2 to their essential doctrinal content." Likewise, J. Feiner, *LThK,* X, p. 571, believes that Gen. 1:26ff., since it was written later, is to be used to interpret Genesis 2.

[51] Cf. H. Haag, "Die Themata der Sündenfall-Geschichte," *Lex tua Veritas*—Festschrift H. Juncker (Trier, 1961), p. 110f., and also "Die Komposition der Sündenfall-Erzählung," *ThQ,* 146 (1966), pp. 1–7.

[52] "Of the 510 times that the word *adam* occurs, it seldom means the individual man or an individual man and not men." *Old Testament Theology* (Philadelphia, 1953), p. 129.

[53] This story too seems to have been originally an independent whole. The change in what God is called indicates this. In the section 3:1–7, *elohim* alone is used 4 times. In the rest of the

Fall story the name *Yahweh-elohim* is always used—twenty times.

[54] Cf. G. von Rad, *Genesis* (Philadelphia, 1961), p. 82f., on Genesis 2: 24.

[55] Cf. the theologians' statements in Part I.

[56] *Banim* "sons" can certainly have the general meaning "children." Probably the word *banim* was intended to be slightly stressed, since for orientals, even today, only sons count.

[57] In any case, A. M. Dubarle, *Le péché originel dans l'Écriture* (Paris, 1958), is expecting too much from the biblical texts when he thinks that in the consequences of sin as described in Genesis 3 "the essential elements of the doctrine of original sin are already present" (p. 69ff.). It is certainly noteworthy that, for the teaching on the preternatural gifts, we depend, in reality, not on scriptural texts but on the Jewish apocryphal writings, especially the *Vita Adae* and the *Apocalypse of Moses*. E. Brandenburger in *Adam und Christus* (Neukirchen, 1962), p. 39, sums up what these two works have to say on this topic as follows: "The place of paradisiacal joy and glory has been taken by trouble and distress (Vit. 1ff., 10; Apoc. 6,9,24), numerous plagues (Apoc. 3), great affliction (9), and great agony (5,6,9,25), great anger and death (14,24). The original dominion of men over animals whose essence was likewise altered, was lost (10 ff., 24)."

[58] Thus V. Hamp, *loc cit.* (cf. n. 14; H. Renckens, *op. cit.*, p. 251f. Both let themselves be led in the final analysis by dogmatic considerations. According to Renckens ". . . we have a divinely willed state of original privilege (immortality) the reality of which is dogmatically certain" (p. 287). For Hamp see note 14. The older generation who easily found the teaching that hereditary death is a hereditary punishment in Genesis 2 may be represented by J. Freundorfer, *Erbsünde und Erbtod beim Apostel Paulus* (Münster i.W., 1927), pp. 8–38.

[59] H. Renckens certainly recognizes this when he says "the

structure of the narrative is homogeneous from top to bottom" (p. 286), but he does not draw the necessary consequences of his statement (cf. n. 57 above).

[60] Cf. A. Weiser, "Die biblische Geschichte vom Paradies und Sündenfall," *Deutsche Theologie* (1937), pp. 9–37—*Glaube und Geschichte im alten Testament* (Göttingen, 1961), pp. 228–257.

[61] Cf. J. A. Soggin, *Bb,* 44 (1963), pp. 524–528: *"La traduzione del nostra passo è dunque la seguente: 'Nel giorno che (o 'qualora') tu ne mangerai (o 'mangiassi'), sarai degno di morte'"* (p. 528). "The translation of our passage is thus as follows: 'on the day that (or 'when') you eat of it, you will deserve to die.'"

[62] V. Hamp, *op. cit.,* p. 104.

[63] Cf. H. Haag, *op. cit.,* (n. 50).

[64] Cf. n. 14.

[65] V. Hamp, *op. cit.,* p. 107. According to Hamp, this passage is thus to be considered only as a literary quotation.

[66] Cf. E. Brandenburger, *op. cit.,* p. 53.

[67] The most remarkable passage is probably 4 Esdras 3: 6–10: "And thou leddest him into paradise, which thy right hand had planted, before even the earth came forward. And unto him thou gavest commandment to love thy way: which he transgressed, and immediately thou appointedst death in him and in his generations . . . And again in process of time thou broughtest the flood upon those who dwelt in the world . . . as death over Adam, so was flood to these." (Translation taken from the Authorized Version.)

[68] E. Brandenburger, *op. cit.,* pp. 53–64.

[69] The word "imagination" (yeser), used here twice, contains an indication of man's weakness and frailty (Ps. 103: 14. Cf. also the use of the corresponding verb *ysr* in Gen. 2:7), in particular an indication of moral weakness and susceptibility (Deut. 31: 21).

[70] K. Rahner, in order to save the historicity (in the aforemen-

tioned sense) of Genesis 2ff., without having to accept a historical tradition about what happened, coined the unhappy phrase, "geschichtliche Aetiologie" ("historical aetiology"). *LThK,* I, 1011f. By this he means the deduction of a historical cause from present circumstances. Cf. N. Lohfink's criticism, "Genesis 2ff. also 'geschichtliche Aetiologie,' " *Schol,* 38 (1963), pp. 321–334: "Outwardly, Rahner's system of concepts simply looks like arbitrary, *a priori,* conclusions," *Ibid.,* p. 328. For another discussion of Rahner's "historical aetiology" see the critical article by L. Alonso Schökel, "Motivos sapienciales y de Alianza en Gen. 2: 3," *Bb,* 43 (1962), pp. 295–316.

[71] Nowhere does scripture say that Jesus died for the sin of Adam, but as early as the Credo of the first community it is proclaimed that he died for "our sins" (I Cor. 15:3) or for those of the "world" (2 Cor. 5: 19). On the *world view* of the fathers of the Council of Trent, cf. the remark of A. Vanneste, *NRTh,* 87 (1956), p. 716 (cf. n. 100): "Il faut . . . rappeler qu'en tant que telle, la question de l'historicité ou de la non-historicité du récit de la chute n'a même pas effleuré les esprits des Pères conciliaires. Au seizième siècle, tous, les catholiques comme les réformateurs, pensaient, 'naïvement' que les choses s'étaient effectivement passées comme elles son présentées dans la Genèse." ("We must . . . remember that the question of the historicity or the unhistoricity of the Fall story as such never suggested itself to the Council Fathers. In the sixteenth century, everyone, reformers as well as Catholics, 'naively' thought that things really happened as they are presented in Genesis.")

[72] K. Rahner does not exclude the possibility that a revelation may have been handed down from the very beginning. *LThK,* I, 1012. H. Renckens, *op. cit.,* p. 39, rightfully remarks about such an idea: "Such imaginative constructions may be given short shrift. To begin with we can say that both the enormous interval of time

which would have had to have been covered by such a tradition, and still more the circumstances of life of the prehistoric human race in which this tradition would have had to have been preserved and handed down make the hypothesis of any kind of tradition whatever, above the purely instinctive or subconcious level, a mere delusion." Since the publication of the German edition of this work, K. Rahner has reversed his position concerning monogenism. He now states: "Monogenism is certainly no dogma." (As quoted by Ignatius Hunt in a review of P. de Rosa's *Original Sin* in CBQ, 29 (1967), p. 614.)

[73] *Loc. cit.,* p. 44.

[74] The only passage which could have been thought of here is the aforementioned Ecclus. 25:24. This passage, however, is concerned with the cause not of sin but of death, and death is not ascribed to Adam but to Eve. A. M. Dubarle (*op. cit.,* p. 101) thus believes that the influence of the Genesis story is of late date; that it is not to be noticed with certainty until the books Tobias, Ecclesiasticus and Wisdom, and that even there a real teaching on original sin was not perceived by the inspired authors of the Old Testament.

[75] This idea, it is generally admitted today, cannot be read into Psalm 51: 7, "Indeed, in guilt was I born, and in sin my mother conceived me." The meaning of this passage is the same as that of Gen. 8: 21. Cf. E. Podechard, *Le Psautier I* (Lyons, 1949), on this verse. Also A. Feuillet, "Le verset 7 du miserere et le péché originel," *RScR,* p. 32 (1944), pp. 5–26.

[76] Cf. J. Scharbert, *Solidarität in Segen und Fluch im alten Testament und im alten Orient I* (Bonn, 1958), and J. de Fraine, *Adam und seine Nachkommen* (Cologne, 1962), pp. 64–97.

[77] Cf. J. de Fraine, *op. cit.,* pp. 123–128.

[78] Cf. W. Eichrodt, *Theologie des Alten Testaments* II–III (Stuttgart⁴, 1961), p. 271.

[79] See P. Lengsfeld, *Adam und Christus* (Essen, 1965): "Whether

biological monogenism represents the only possibility for the dogmatic utilization of the relationship of one to all may well be doubted
since the text contains no teaching about descent; it does not even
hint at such a teaching" (p. 85 n. 255).

[80] K. H. Schelkle, *Meditationen über den Römerbrief* (Einsiedeln, 1962), *loc. cit.*

[81] This view is held as certain by (among others) J. Cambier,
"Péchés des hommes et péché d'Adam en Rom. 5: 12," *New Testament Studies* (1965), pp. 217–255: *"La description de la situation
religieuse ancienne sera plutôt une appréciation théologique de
celle-ci; l'apôtre, cela va de soi, empruntera les représentations littéraires de sa composition au canevas de l'histoire primitive, cette
dernière étant elle-même une affirmation théologique exprimée en
langue populaire. Leur utilisation par S. Paul ne confère évidem-
ment à ce cadre et à ces représentations aucune valeur d'histoire, au
sens moderne du mot, pas plus que l'utilisation de l'image de Jonas
par le Christ en vue de prédire mystérieusement sa résurrection ne
confère le caractère d'historicité aux représentations littéraires mises
en oeuvre dans le beau livre prophétique de Jonas"* (p. 224). ("A
description of the ancient religious situation must be, rather, a
theological appreciation of it. The apostle, it goes without saying,
borrows the literary representations for the composition on his
canvas from primitive history; but that history itself is a theological
affirmation expressed in popular language. The fact that Saint Paul
uses them certainly does not confer historical value on this framework or on these representations, in the modern sense of the word
"history," any more than Christ's use of the image of Jonah for
a mystical prediction of his resurrection confers historicity on the
literary presentations used in the beautiful prophetic book of
Jonah.")

[82] Cf. E. Brandenburg, *op. cit.*, p. 161: "The middle stage was
consciously excluded in standard late Jewish views because they

rejected every influence of Adam that would affect the essence of man; namely, his relation to God."

[83] "The power of sin entered into the cosmos like a ruler." O. Kuss, *Der Römerbrief* (Regenburg, 1963), p. 227.

[84] It is incomprehensible that A. M. Dubarle can speak of a *heritage, op. cit.,* pp. 167–170. For the same reason, it is impossible to agree in finding here a teaching of "inherited death." Cf. K. H. Schelkle, *loc. cit.;* O. Kuss *op. cit.,* p. 231. *"Le verbe dielthen ne décrit pas le passage de la Mort à travers les générations des hommes, encore moins une mort transmise de génération en génération par hérédité; il signifie que la Mort atteint tous les hommes, tous soumis à la domination de la puissance mauvaise."* J. Cambier, *op. cit.,* p. 252. "The verb dielthen does not describe the passage of death from one generation of men to another, much less a death transmitted from generation to generation by heredity; it means that death reaches everyone, that all are subject to the dominion of this evil power."

[85] Recent commentators offer the following translations for dielthen: *"la mort a atteint tous les hommes"* M. J. Lagrange (Paris, 1931), A. Viard (Paris, 1951); *"la mort s'est répandue sur tous les hommes"* F. J. Leenhardt (Neuchâtel, 1957); *"und so der Tod zu allen Menschen hindurchdrang,"* P. Althaus (Göttingen, 1959); *"und so zu allen Menschen der Tod durchdrang,"* H. W. Schmidt (Berlin, 1962); *"und so der Tod auf alle Menschen sich ausbreitete,"* O. Michel (Göttingen,[12] 1963); *am besten, wie mir scheint,* O. Kuss (Regensburg,[2] 1963) *"und so zu allen Menschen der Tod hinkam,"* W. Bauer, *Griech deutsches Worterbuch zu den schriften des Neuen Testament und der übrigen altchristlichen Literatur* (Berlin,[5] 1958) gives *"hinkommen, hingelangen"* as the meaning of dierchomai in this passage.

[86] J. Cambier, *op. cit.,* p. 234f.

[87] *"L'apôtre ne songe pas au seul aspect temporel de la mort,*

mais d'abord à celle-ci en tant précisément qu'elle est privation du salut." ("The apostle is not thinking here only of the temporal aspect of death; he is thinking of death primarily as loss of salvation.") S. Lyonnet, "Le péché originel et l'exégèse de Rom. 5: 12–14", *RScR,* 44 (1956), pp. 63–84; here p. 66.

[88] In I. Cor. 15: 21f., Paul sees death in the light of the final victory of God's kingdom. (Cf. v. 28.)

[89] L. Ligier, *Péché d'Adam et péché du monde* (Paris, 1960–61), II, p. 270f., and n. 60, has collected the various translations proposed by S. Lyonnet: *"sous la condition que, . . . de,"* Bb (1955), *"à la condition que, . . . de"* (ibid.) *"moyennant le fait que"* (ibid.) *"vu le fait que,"* RScR (1956), *"selon que"* (ibid.), *"en tant que, dans la mesure où"* (ibid.), *"étant remplie la condition que"* (ibid.). In addition: *DBS,* VII, p. 546, *"du fait que"* (*Bible de Jérusalem*). J. Cambier, *op. cit.,* pp. 242–249 makes a new proposal that the antecedent of the relative pronoun is Adam and he translates: "on account of whom."

[90] *"Pour les Grecs . . . , à peu d'exceptions près, l'Apôtre vise ici les péchés personnels des adultes; tel est en effet le sens que le verbe hemarton offre toujours chez saint Paul, comme dans toute la Bible, et notamment dans la formule 'tous ont péché' employée quelques page auparavant (3:23)."* S. Lyonnet, *RScR,* 44 (1956), p. 68. ("For the Greeks . . . , with few exceptions, the apostle here has in mind personal sins of adults. Such is, in fact, the sense that the verb hemarton always has in Paul as in the entire Bible, and notably in the formula, 'all have sinned' used some pages earlier.") "The awkward 'for all have sinned' (hemarton; cf. Rom. 3: 23) cannot be done away with by violence" O. Kuss, *op. cit.,* p. 231. Also, J. Cambier, who translates eph ho with "on account of whom," translates the passage "on account of whom all have sinned," not "have become sinful." (*Ibid.*). In any case, Adam remains the cause

of the personal sins of his descendants. L. Ligier, *op. cit.,* II, p. 275f., has tried to show that in the Septuagint the verb hamartano can indicate a condition, but it certainly does not have this meaning in the principle passage that Ligier uses for proof, Isaiah 24: 6.

[91] This understanding is presented by K. H. Schelkle as follows: "With ways of thinking that he had learned in the school of Jewish theology, Paul shows that death was transmitted to mankind by virtue of their physical descent from Adam and as their inheritance. Through his transgression of the command given in Paradise, Adam drew upon himself the punishment of death. After that Israel had no command or law until Moses. From Adam to Moses sin certainly existed, but during this period transgressions were never punishable by death. Nevertheless, between Adam and Moses, men died. They did not die because they deserved death by virtue of the law, but their death was the consequence of the first sin of the individual Adam" *op. cit.,* p. 79f. O. Michel comments on Romans 5: 13f., "Our meditation will consider the childhood of the human race between Adam and Moses with respect to the understanding of the law. In this period sin is an independent power in the history of humanity, but it has not yet been imputed, written down, charged to them. In the history of this childhood there were general and special judgments of God, but only since the law was given on Sinai has the severer judgment over men existed. In a certain sense our verse develops the thesis of Rom. 4:15. Even when men have not sinned in the same way as Adam they are subject to death" (*loc. cit.*).

[92] *RScR,* 44 (1956), pp. 75–84; *DBS,* VII, pp. 551–558.

[93] 4: 15, however, has a completely different theme.

[94] Also see J. Cambier, p. 273, n. 1.

[95] O. Kuss, *op. cit.,* p. 233. Likewise, one cannot agree with P. Lengsfeld when he, citing O. Kuss, writes: "Understanding every

state of sin in the past as hereditary sin, as a state of sin inherited from Adam, brings out, without doubt, the meaning of the Pauline statements" (*op. cit.*, p. 118).

⁹⁶ Cf. J. Cambier, *op. cit.*, p. 227.

⁹⁷ *Lambano* often has the sense in the New Testament of accepting something offered; e.g., Matt. 13: 20 and parallel, John 12: 48, 17: 8 (the Word), John 3: 11, 32f., I John 5: 9 (the witness).

⁹⁸ Cf. S. Lyonnet, *DBS,* VII, p. 559; E. Brandenburger, *op. cit.*, pp. 230, 242f.

⁹⁹ *Hamartolai katestathesan,* v. 19, means simply "they became sinners." Cf. F. Zorell, *Lexicon Graecum Novi Testamenti* (Paris, 1931), p. 636: peccatores facti sunt multi." Thus when P. Lengsfeld comments on this passage, "Before committing a conscious and responsible act, the man who opens his eyes in this world finds himself already a sinner, *op cit.*, p. 104, and when O. Kuss says, "Man does not *become* a sinner, but he finds himself in this world already a sinner; he is a sinner from the start," *op. cit.*, p. 244, then they read their own presuppositions into the text.

¹⁰⁰ *Paulus Lehrer der Väter* (Düsseldorf, 1956), pp. 162–196.

¹⁰¹ Schelkle, *op cit.*, p. 174 (emphasis added).

¹⁰² "À Propos de Romains 5: 12 dans l'oeuvre de S. Augustin," *Bb,* 45 (1964), p. 541. H. Rondet, "Le péché originel dans la tradition. De Clément de Rome à saint Irénée," *Bulletin de Littérature Ecclésiatique* (1965), pp. 241–271, has recently shown that neither the Apostolic Fathers nor the apologists paid any particular attention to the fifth chapter of Romans.

¹⁰³ Pope Zosimus, a Greek, in complete and conscious agreement with this reading, did not feel inclined to subscribe to the theology peculiar to Africa and Augustine which burdened the unbaptized child with true original sin. Zosimus' predecessor, Innocent, thought it necessary to free the child from *perditio*. Zosimus conceded that it was necessary to be freed from a death (*mors*), not primarily

physical death, through the grace of Christ at Baptism. But the Pope, in opposition to the Africans, refused to accept original sin. In addition, see F. Floëri, "Le péché originel d'après Zosime et Augustin," *Augustinus Magister II* (Paris, 1954), pp. 755–761.

[104] Cf. S. Lyonnet, "Rom. V, 12 chez Saint Augustin," *Mélanges de Lubac I* (Paris, 1963), pp. 327–339), here p. 328. Also see J. Gross, *op. cit.,* 1, p. 304f.

[105] VI, 12, 39; *PL,* 44, p. 843.

[106] Cf. A. Vanneste, "La préhistoire du décret du Concile de Trente sur le péché originel," *NRTh,* 86 (1964), pp. 490–510. Also "Le Décret du Concile de Trente sur le péché originel," *ibid.,* 87 (1965), pp. 688–726.

[107] *Conc. Trid. ed. Soc. Goerr V,* p. 166.

[108] Cf. A. Vanneste, *NRTh,* 87 (1965), pp. 691–694.

[109] Cf. A. Vanneste, *op. cit.,* p. 713.

[110] L. Scheffczyk, "Die Auslegung der Heilige Schrift als dogmatische Aufgabe," *MüThZ,* 15 (1964), pp. 190–204, here p. 191 (emphasis added).

[111] As mentioned above (p. 69) this canon takes up the second canon of Orange which states that Adam's sin injured not only himself but also his posterity, and that through one man, not only physical death was transmitted (*transiisse*) as punishment for sin to the entire human race, but also sin itself as the death of the soul. As we know from the Augustinian polemic against the Pelagians, the council was concerned in the second part of the sentence with the idea that through the first sin not only physical death but sin itself was transmitted (*transiisse*) to all mankind. The council was not concerned about how this transmission took place.

[112] Cf. "Haereses super peccato originali, lectae in generali congregatione die 9. iunii 1546." *Conc. Trid. ed. Soc. Goerr.,* V, p. 212f.: "*Septimus est Pelagii, peccatum originale esse praevarica-*

tionis Adae imitationem." ("The seventh error of Pelagius is that he says that original sin is the imitation of Adam's fault.") For this teaching of Pelagius, cf. *DThC*, XII, p. 683. With this statement the council scarcely wanted to exclude the idea that the sin of Adam is *also* extended through *imitatio*. Several council fathers wished the formulation *"non imitatione sola"* ("not by mere imitation") or *"non solum imitatione"* ("not only by imitation"), *ibid.*, pp. 202f., 209. A. Vanneste, *op. cit.*, p. 719, remarks on the formula *"propagatione, non imitatione transfusum" "C'était en quelque sorte l'expression la plus typique du pélagianisme, tel qu'Augustin le décrit. En fait, il est plutôt étonnant d'avoir dû attendre le seizième siècle pour qu'elle devienne l'objet d'une condamnation officielle de la part de l'Église. Le devons-nous au désir des Pères de se laver de tout soupçon de pélagianisme, ou est-ce plutôt l'interprétation pélagienne qu'avait donnée Erasme de Rom. 5 qui a déclenché la réaction du Concile?"* ("It was, in a way, the most typical expression of Pelagianism as Augustine describes it. In fact, it is astonishing to have had to wait until the sixteenth century for it to become the object of an official condemnation by the Church. Do we owe it to the Fathers' desire to cleanse themselves from every suspicion of Pelagianism, or was it Erasmus' Pelagian interpretation of Romans 5 which brought on the council's reaction?"

[113] The formulation of Canon 3: *"Adae peccatum, quod origine unum est et . . . omnibus inest unicuique proprium"* ("The sin of Adam which is of one origin and . . . is in all, peculiar to each") is directed against the teaching of the Netherland theologian, Pigge (*Pighius*), according to which the one sin of Adam is only *attributed* to his posterity. With the words *"quod origine unum est,"* the council affirms the truth in Pigge's teaching; with the words *"omnibus inest unicuique proprium,"* the council states that the sin of Adam, in spite of its singularity of origin, is multiplied in

his posterity. No information about the *way* in whch Adam's sin was continued can be gained from this formulation. Neither can a teaching of monogenism be deduced from it because this problem was completely unknown to the council. Cf. A. Vanneste, *op. cit.*, pp. 723, and 155.

[114] In the council's text, "peccata mundi."